VIRGINIA WOOLF AND BLOOMSBURY

BY

IRMA RANTAVAARA

THE FOLCROFT PRESS INC. /1970

Limited to 150 Copies

SUOMALAISEN TIEDEAKATEMIAN TOIMITUKSIA
ANNALES ACADEMIÆ SCIENTIARUM FENNICÆ

SARJA - SER. B *NIDE - TOM.* 82,1

VIRGINIA WOOLF AND BLOOMSBURY

BY
IRMA RANTAVAARA

HELSINKI 1953

*Presented for publication in the Annales Academiae Fennicae
at the meeting of the Academy on January 9, 1953,
by Rafael Koskimies and Y. M. Biese.*

Helsinki 1953
Printed by Suomalaisen Kirjallisuuden Seuran Kirjapainon Oy.

Contents

Chap.		Page
	Acknowledgements	5
I.	A Bloomsbury Lady in the Making	7
II.	To Bloomsbury via Cambridge	26
III.	The Atmosphere of Bloomsbury	44
IV.	Bloomsbury To-day	62
V.	Father and Daughter as Critics	68
VI.	First Novels	81
VII.	Virginia Woolf Finds Herself	91
VIII.	Mrs. Dalloway	105
IX.	To the Lighthouse	112
X.	Orlando	131
XI.	A Room of One's Own and Three Guineas	139
XII.	The Waves and After	150
	Bibliography	161
	Index	168

Acknowledgements

When taking part in a British Council Summer Course at Oxford in 1947, I was amused and interested to hear how greatly the lecturers there differed in their opinions concerning the group of writers and artists known as Bloomsbury. My curiosity was aroused to discover exactly what Bloomsbury is, for there seemed to be no reliable and thorough interpretation of the word. When I was granted the Rockefeller Foundation Fellowship in 1949—50, I was able for one year to pursue my research at the British Museum and in Cambridge. As I progressed with my work, I came to realize that Bloomsbury cannot be properly understood without a comprehension of Virginia Woolf. Thus my work grew into a study on her, especially in her relation to her intimate circle of friends and the ideas they imbibed in Cambridge.

My sincere thanks are due to Dr. Rafael Koskimies, Professor of World Literature and Aesthetics at the University of Helsinki, who took an interest in my project and, through the mediation of the Humanities Faculty of the University of Helsinki, recommended me for a Rockefeller Foundation Fellowship, without which this result of my studies would not be in existence. Mr. F. L. Lucas, Fellow of King's College, Cambridge, was kind enough to read through my manuscript and give me valuable counsel. Indeed, the monthly talks I had with him were, for a foreigner who was thus permitted contact with a Cambridge mind, a pleasure and an inspiration of a rare kind. The memory will be a treasure for life. Mr. Leonard Woolf also took an interest in my work, giving me helpful hints and valuable information, for which I want to thank him most sincerely.

As for the financial help, in addition to expressing my gratitude for the generosity of the Rockefeller Foundation, it is my pleasant duty to acknowledge a grant from the Wihuri Fund, Helsinki, towards the publication of this book, as well as smaller grants, in 1948, from the Finnish Ministry of Education and from the Canadian Association of University Women. My thanks are also due to the Academia Scientiarum Fennica for the honour of including this volume in their *Annales*.

Helsinki, April 10, 1953.

IRMA RANTAVAARA

I

A Bloomsbury Lady in the Making

In *The Voyage Out*, Virginia Woolf's first novel, Helen Ambrose, the scholar's wife, has a certain black book on her table. From a quotation we deduce that book to be Prof. G. E. Moore's *Principia Ethica*, at one time a very important book indeed, little short of a Bible, for people who wanted to know all about the real values in life, of good, of truth, of the good states of mind, in short, of the ends as opposed to the means. Now, if a lady keeps *Principia Ethica* by her bed, she is, unless she is a bad sleeper and wants to drug herself by reading the book, clearly one of those who, according to Virginia Woolf's delightfully sweeping definition of a lady, desire Mozart and Einstein, i.e. pursue ends and not means. In the same novel we also meet for the first time Clarissa Dalloway. She is described as a peer's daughter, married to an M. P., a shallow creature who only cares for what is fashionable and the latest craze. So, she cannot be counted as one of our ladies. The later Clarissa Dalloway, of whose day in June, engaged in preparations for her party, we get such a charming picture, hardly cared for deeper intellectual pleasures either, except when she wanted to show off as a fashionable hostess in furtherance of her husband's career. Katherine Hilbery, in *Night and Day*, solved mathematical problems in the secrecy of her room while openly occupied in writing her literary grandfather's biography. She obviously has at least one foot on the right side of the barricade. Mrs. Ramsay, in *To the Lighthouse*, would, we feel sure, also have liked more time for dealing with ends, but her tiresome husband and eight children kept her busy with means. And so on. With all Virginia Woolf's imaginary women, you come to see that the ladies of her definition are heiresses of intellectual rather than material fortunes.

But the latter must not be excluded. On the contrary, we are told expressly that a room of one's own and five hundred pounds a year are the basic rations needed in the journey towards becoming a lady.

In the nineteenth century the English society was still neatly divided. »There is aristocracy; the landed gentry; the professional class; the commercial class; the working class; and there, in one dark blot, is that great class which is called simply and comprehensively 'The Poor'. To the nineteenth-century writer human life must have looked like a landscape cut up into separate fields. In each field was gathered a different group of people.»[1] Virginia Woolf more or less accepts that division on the material side of life. But in the spiritual field of Mrs. Woolf's vision these groups gradually get mixed and divided again into different sets of people whom we may for our purposes term highbrows, middlebrows, and lowbrows, consisting of both sexes and beginning to consist of people from all stations of life. Virginia Woolf herself is confessedly a highbrow; she makes no bones about it: »I ask nothing better than that all reviewers, for ever, and everywhere, should call me a highbrow. I will do my best to oblige them. If they like to add Bloomsbury, W. C. 1, that is the correct postal address, and my telephone number is in the Directory. But if your reviewers, or any other reviewer, dares hint that I live in South Kensington, I will sue him for libel. If any human being, man, woman, or dog, cat or a half-crushed worm dares call me 'middlebrow' I will take my pen and stab him, dead.»[2] Elsewhere she defines the middlebrows as »the fashionable intellectuals — who like to have the latest book on their tables».[3] They are below all criticism, unworthy of any attention, despicable beings, better dead. With lowbrows the matter is different. They are honest, at any rate, and that is all that counts. They are to be pitied, but not despised, for they are victims of their circumstances. However, it is »much better to be a lady». The advantages are obvious: »We have as much to give them (the working classes) as they to give us — wit and detachment,

---

[1] *The Moment and Other Essays*, pp. 108—9
[2] *The Death of the Moth*, p. 119
[3] *The Voyage Out*, p. 264

learning and poetry, and all those good gifts which those who have never answered bells or minded machines enjoy by right. — One could not be Mrs. Giles of Durham because one's body has never stood at the washtub; one's hands have never wrung and scrubbed and chopped up whatever the meat may be that makes a miner's supper. The picture therefore was always letting in irrelevancies. One sat in an armchair or read a book. One saw landscapes and seascapes, perhaps Greece or Italy, where Mrs. Giles or Mrs. Edwards must have seen slag heaps and rows upon rows of slate-roofed houses. — Certainly there were no armchairs, or electric light, or hot water laid on in their lives, no Greek hills or Mediterranean bays in their dreams. Bakers and butchers did not call for orders. They did not sign a cheque to pay the weekly bills, or order, over the telephone, a cheap but quite adequate seat at the Opera.»[4]

It now becomes obvious that Virginia Woolf is of the opinion which Bagehot put into words by saying: »A man's wife is his fault, his mother is his misfortune», applied to fathers and husbands as well. You cannot really have the best of life, if you have not the means to enjoy the ends, and yet you must not be bothered with means, because then you waste your precious moments! The only solution of this complicated problem is to have a father — or an aunt, like Virginia — who leaves you some money. But not too much, mind you. Money must not have any hold on you, therefore it is best to have just enough for a comfortable life without pecuniary worries. But money is not enough either. You must also be born into a family of certain cultural standards.

In her essay on Robinson Crusoe Virginia Woolf further stresses the importance of getting the writer's perspective right, of understanding »in what order he ranges the large common objects upon which novelists are fated to gaze: man and men; behind them Nature and above them that power which for convenience and brevity we may call God.»[5] She also points out how much influence circumstances have upon opinions. »If Godwin had been brought up in the precincts

---

[4] Intr. Letter in *Life As We Have Known It*, p. XXVI
[5] *The Common Reader II*, p. 52

of the Temple and had drunk deep of antiquity and old letters at Christ's Hospital, he might never have cared a straw for the future of man and his rights in general. If Jane Austen had lain as a child on the landing to prevent her father from thrashing her mother, her soul might have burnt with such a passion against tyranny that all her novels might have been consumed in one cry for justice.»[6] Although life does not necessarily always work on such clear-cut lines, we are entitled to conclude that Virginia Woolf herself would probably have been a different kind of writer, had she not been able to call herself — with a smile lurking round the corners of her sensitive mouth — »an unmitigated snob», a highbrow and a lady.

In *The Voyage Out* many little glimpses of Ridley Ambrose, a scholar and a former Cambridge don, now residing in London editing classics, and his delightful wife, Helen, can be safely read as inspired by the Stephen household. »'It's books', sighed Helen, lifting an armful of sad volumes from the floor to the shelf. Greek from morning to night. If ever Miss Rachel marries, pray that she may marry a man who doesn't know his ABC!»[7] Leslie Stephen's books too, were »sad volumes», lying scattered about, dog-eared, full of drawings and underlinings. He, too, knew his Greek, but in other things depended on a good deal of attention and mothering. The half-bantering, half-serious tone that Mrs. Ambrose has to assume to brighten up the moods of her sometimes morose husband was undoubtedly often heard in the Stephen household where the whole family had not infrequently to refuse to take the father seriously until his mood of depression was dispelled. There were — we feel sure — a great many brisk arguments between husband and wife in the jocular vein of one in *The Voyage Out* »as to whether he was or was not wholly ignored by the entire civilized world. 'Considering the last batch', said Helen, 'you deserve beating. You were asked to lecture, you were offered a degree, and some silly woman

---

[6] ibid., p. 157
[7] *The Voyage Out*, p. 27

praised not only your books but your beauty — she said you are what
Shelley would have been if Shelley had lived to fifty-five and grown
a beard. Really, Ridley, I think you're the vainest man I know — —
which I may tell you is saying a good deal . . .'»[8] There is playful
tenderness and great affection in the picture, just as there was in the
Stephen family where eight children grew up into man- and womanhood. So indiscriminating was the affection that it would have been
very difficult for a stranger to know that there were three different
lots of children among them, both parents having married twice.
Leslie Stephen had gone through a great deal of happiness and still
more unhappiness before he was »fifty-five and had grown a beard»,
like Ridley Ambrose, or had begun to remind you of »Phoebus Apollo
turned fasting friar», as George Meredith put it in his *Egoist*[9] where
Vernon Whitford »with his devotion to the cold idea of duty», his
sombre looks, but infectious humour, with his leanness »like a fork
with the wind whistling through the prongs», with his »unbearable»
eyes that »dwelt in the memory as if they had left a phosphorescent
line», undoubtedly bears close resemblance to the author's great
friend Leslie Stephen. An altogether pleasant picture it is; in that,
too, like its origin.

Leslie Stephen [10] was born on November 28, 1832, and grew into
a delicate, sensitive, highly-strung child, easily excited, affectionate,
fond of flowers and animals, and of poetry, the reading of which,
when he was about ten years old, was considered dangerous for him
by the family-physician. »The Last Days of Pompeii», we read in
his mother's diary, »caused the colour to rise in his cheeks, he was
trembling and almost crying.»[11] In his ninth year there was an incident
which shows the later Leslie Stephen in the making: because the boy
was easily fatigued, his parents wanted him to ride to church on the

---

[8] idem

[9] ch. VI, p. 35

[10] This chapter was written at the end of 1949, two years before the publication of Noel Annan's admirable book on Leslie Stephen.

[11] Maitland, III. 27

donkey, but, says his mother in her diary, Leslie was »greatly distressed at the idea, and said that he thought it wrong to make the donkey work on Sunday».[12] There seems indeed never to have been a time when Leslie was not listening to his very strict conscience.

For at least three generations the Stephens had shown leanings towards legal as well as literary occupations. They had a somewhat heavy-going but clear kind of style which we find also in Leslie's writings, though moulded into something less ponderous. As examples may be mentioned *Considerations on Imprisonment for Debt*, by James Stephen (d. 1779), *War in Disguise* by his son, Leslie's grandfather (d. 1832), *Essays in Ecclesiastical Biography* by Leslie's father, the Right Hon. Sir James Stephen, K. C. B. (d. 1859). In the whole family there glowed a certain fiery spark which flared if there was some humanitarian campaign to be sponsored or religious doctrines to be defended. Both Leslie's grandfather and father were abolitionists and strictly evangelical. His grandfather took Wilberforce's sister for his second wife, and was thus doubly connected with the movement. Both Leslie's parents belonged to the Clapham Sect or »The Saints». His mother was the daughter of John Venn, Rector of Clapham. The five Stephen children thus grew up in an atmosphere permeated by religion but relieved by tolerance and humour. In that respect their home differed totally from Butler's or Gosse's. Between Leslie and his father there was an unfailing devotion, even though later their opinions differed entirely. In the Stephen family there was no pressing, as we read in the father's journal: »I have never yet passed a day without praying for the spiritual weal of my children, since I had any to pray for, and if we err on the side of not pressing them to religious demonstrations, developments of early sensibility, may God forgive us, and compensate the loss to them! My daily and nightly terror is that they should be 'patent Christians' — formalists, praters, cheats, without meaning or even knowing it.»[13] The father's prayer was heard; but, as so often happens with prayers, in a way he did not mean.

[12] idem
[13] Maitland. II. 8

The children grew up surrounded, too, by culture and taste. James Stephen had been educated at Trinity Hall, Cambridge, was later appointed permanent counsel to the Board of Trade, assistant Under-Secretary of State for the Colonies, and, in 1836, Under-Secretary. In 1849 he returned to his old college in Cambridge as Regius Professor of Modern History. Leslie entered it in 1850 taking his degree with honours in mathematics in 1854. Leslie's brother, James Fitzjames, studied law, and in time became a judge of the High Court of Justice and was knighted. Leslie himself chose Holy Orders, as he could thus try for a clerical fellowship at his college and become a don, financially independent of his father. He did so and stayed at Cambridge for fourteen years. The sickly child had developed into a man, lean, it is true, but vigorous, a great walker, an enthusiastic climber of the Alps and »a fanatical oarsman». His intellectual notability later in life came as a surprise to many who had known him at Cambridge. His athletic interests made him very popular among the undergraduates who appreciated his friendly, unorthodox attitude. Brusque in speech, he had a very kind heart which made him greatly loved. »His university life», writes the Rev. F. F. Kelly, Vicar of Camberwell, who had been undergraduate in Stephen's time, »was a grand life of doing good to men at a critical time. — Pretty nearly any of us in those days would have done anything for Stephen.»[14]

The life of a don in those days was extremely pleasant. The number of students, especially at Trinity Hall, was very small, 41, to be exact. There was plenty of leisure with pleasant company at your disposal. In his *Life of Henry Fawcett* as well as in the *Sketches from Cambridge by a Don*, Leslie Stephen draws a lively picture of the Cambridge that was only a little less than a hundred years ago. Typical Cambridge men were, we are told, »believers in hard facts and figures, admirers of strenuous common sense, and hearty despisers of sentimentalism. — At the period (round 1850—60) the more sentimental youth learnt Tennyson by heart, wept over Jane

---

[14] ibid., V. 59

Eyre, and was beginning to appreciate Browning. If more seriously disposed, he read *Sartor Resartus* and the *French Revolution*, he followed the teachings of Maurice and had some leaning to Christian Socialism. But the sterner utilitarians looked to Mill as their great prophet. They repudiated Carlyle as reactionary and set down Maurice as muddle-headed.»[15] Stephen himself read a great deal, as is shown by the list he made, the length of which would have surprised even his friends, had they seen it. The books mostly dealt with philosophy and political economy or history. There are surprisingly few works on theology, but Comte was included and proved important. Conversation was then an integral part of university life in Cambridge as well as Oxford. »The essence of university life is laughter and the love of friends», is Stephen's definition. »Sleep seemed an impertinent interruption to a permanent flow of conversation.»[16] The topics were of different weight: gossip, Civil War in America, extension of the franchise, Utilitarianism, the utterances of Cobden, Palmerston, Gladstone, Disraeli. Religious controversies (such as the Oxford Movement) stirred little interest here. The epithet 'Evangelical' generally connoted contempt, Stephen tells us. »Though we could lose our temper over political discussions, we became calm when conversation was turned to the controversies which divided the religious world. We left such matters to Oxford.»[17]

The experts claim that there is a special spirit in Cambridge different from that of Oxford and that it is, for instance, »impossible to imagine a Matthew Arnold who had never been at Oxford and a Leslie Stephen who had never been at Cambridge.»[18] Oxford, we are told, cares more for the graces, Cambridge, for cold reason. Leslie Stephen's analysis of his kindred spirits confirms the statement: »Even when Cambridge men took to the study of classical literature, they stuck to good, tangible matters of grammatical construction without bothering themselves about purely literary or

---

[15] *Life of Henry Fawcett*, p. 23
[16] ibid., p. 87
[17] *Some Early Impressions*, p. 56
[18] MacCarthy: *Leslie Stephen*, p. 23

philosophical interests. They did not deny the existence of the soul, but knew that it should be kept in its proper place. It may be an estimable entity, but it also generates 'fads' and futile enthusiasm and gushing sentimentalism. It should not be unduly stimulated in early years but kept in due subordination to the calm understanding occupied with positive matters of fact.»[19] From that utterance we can anticipate what was to follow.

He had been ordained priest in 1859. Some of his friends had warned him, feeling that he had no serious call. But Leslie wanted to obey his father's wish, especially because it made him financially independent and made his stay in Cambridge possible. The religious duties of a clerical don consisted of reading a prayer and delivering a sermon every now and then. But there came a moment when his honesty and sincerity, the Venn and Stephen element in him, would not allow him to continue uttering texts he did not believe in. »I read Comte, too, (besides other books) and became convinced, among other things, that Noah's flood was a fiction (or rather convinced that I had never believed in it) and that it was wrong for me to read the story as if it were the sacred truth.»[20] Consequently he resigned his fellowship, which meant that he had to leave his beloved Cambridge and to enter a new field of activity at the age of thirty-three. He hoped to settle down in London as a journalist. His brother had by that time made a name in criticism also, and Leslie hoped that his brother's contacts would help him. They did.

On January 26, 1865, after having left Cambridge, Leslie wrote in his diary very characteristically: »I now believe in nothing, to put it shortly; but I do not the less believe in morality etc. etc. I mean to live and die a gentleman if possible».[21] Truth and virtue became his religion. It is not surprising to find that he handles Bishop Butler very admiringly in the *History of English Thought in the Eighteenth Century* as the Bishop holds that the secret of the

---

[19] ibid., p. 33
[20] Maitland, VIII. 133
[21] ibid., VIII. 144

universe is revealed, so far it is revealed, through morality. »A vigorous morality is by its nature one aspect of strong vitality», Stephen again writes in *An Agnostic's Apology*.[22] He became an Agnostic — the term itself is credited to Prof. Huxley, but it was made known generally by Leslie Stephen's writings, especially by his *Essays on Free-Thinking and Plain-Speaking* (1873) and *An Agnostic's Apology* (1893), the Agnostic being »one who asserts that there are limits to the sphere of human intelligence. He asserts, further, what many theologians have expressly maintained, that those limits are such as to exclude at least what Lewes called 'metempirical' knowledge. But he goes further, and asserts, in opposition to theologians, that theology lies within this forbidden sphere.»[23] Further on Stephen characteristically underlines the importance of reason as the only criterion. »Reason, however weak, is our sole guide.»[24] And again: »Man knows nothing of the Infinite and Absolute and, knowing nothing, he had better not be dogmatic about his ignorance!»[25]

In 1865 Stephen started his literary career by writing for the *Saturday Review*, then the *Pall Mall Gazette* and the (New York) *Nation*, as well as for *Frazer's* and the *Fortnightly*. The *Cornhill*, to which he contributed under the nom-de-plume A Cynic, became his main forum from 1866. In 1871 he was made editor of the *Cornhill* and this post he held till 1882 when he took up editing the *Dictionary of National Biography*. For nine years he was the leader of that gigantic enterprise which consisted, when it was finished in 1900, of 29,120 articles written by 653 contributors in 63 volumes covering 29,108 pages. 378 of the articles on leading men of letters and philosophers were written by Leslie Stephen himself.

Apart from his weekly reviewing and editing Stephen had time and energy to write a large number of books dealing mainly with literary and philosophical subjects. It is as if, once having found out that he could write — and he was about thirty before he began

---

[22] ibid., p. 46
[23] ibid., p. 1
[24] ibid., p. 8
[25] ibid., p. 26

to suspect this — he had been carried away with the knowledge. He had so much to say, especially about religion in his newly formulated agnosticism. In politics he was a Liberal with radical tendencies, a disciple of Cobden, Bright, and Mill. The forty years between 1860 and 1900 were exciting in their wealth of new ideas. Darwin's *Origin of Species* as well as Mill's *Liberty* had appeared in 1859. Carlyle, Ruskin, Newman, F. D. Maurice, and Kingsley were followed in their turn by Butler, Shaw, and the Fabians. The Boer War and the Imperialism of Kipling were approaching. There were sides to take and to defend. In his central book, *Science of Ethics* (1882), Stephen adopted the Utilitarian creed coloured with Darwinian ideas of Evolution. In his thinking, whether concerning religious, literary, or politico-economic matters, he applied the Cambridge characteristics: sound reason and cold analysis were to be the basis of opinions. Metaphysics, consequently, did not attract him, and in his literary criticisms he tried to avoid theorizing. His critical method is described in an essay on Charlotte Brontë: »Our literary, like our religious, creed should rest upon a purely rational ground, and be exposed to logical tests. Our faith in an author must, in the first instance, be the product of instinctive sympathy, instead of deliberate reason. It may be propagated by the contagion of enthusiasm, and preached with all the fervour of proselytism. But when we are seeking to justify our emotions, we must endeavour to get for the time into the position of an independent spectator, applying with rigid impartiality such methods as are best calculated to free us from the influence of personal bias.»[26] Whether his constant harping on »freeing oneself from personal bias» and »justifying one's emotions» proved, in the long run, beneficent for his art and insight as a critic, is a matter of opinion, for too great a detachment has its dangers. That it resulted in »soundness» of criticism, no one denies.

In 1863 Stephen made his first trip to America where he was to return again about ten years later. He came home a firm friend of some of the best »Yankees», and one of the first English inter-

---

[26] *Hours in a Library III*, p. 326 (1879)

preters of American mentality, more sympathetic than Dickens in his *Notes*, and at least as searching as Mrs. Trollope and Thackeray. His analysis of American Humour appeared in the *Cornhill Magazine* of January, 1866. He remained a life-long friend of C. E. Norton, J. R. Lowell, and Oliver Wendell Holmes, with whom he corresponded diligently, to the gratification of the biographers, who from those letters get valuable material for their picture of Stephen in joy and sorrow.

In 1866 we read in a letter to Oliver Wendell Holmes of what must have come as a surprise to him as well as to Leslie's other friends, as it can be said to have been a shock to Leslie himself: »— — You therefore will not be surprised at discovering that I am not such a don but that I can fall in love, and you will appreciate the addition which this engagement makes to my happiness, or rather its lift of me from discontent and growling into the purest happiness.»[27] Stephen, who had not thought himself »a marrying man», found ideal happiness in his marriage with Thackeray's younger daughter. Just as he had, as it were, accidentally found out that he could write, he found out now, as he wrote to Prof. Henry Sidgwick, that »all real happiness (after that which depends upon the stomach) consists in the domestic and friendly affections . . .».[28] But the happiness was soon to end. In 1875 his wife died suddenly, and Leslie was left alone with his five-year-old daughter Laura. After that blow Stephen was never quite the same again, for he was a man essentially dependent on love and affection. He began to suffer from bad headaches, was a prey to bitter and sarcastic moods and spells of depression. His only outlet was in writing. »Yet honestly», he writes to C. E. Norton on March 5, 1876, »literature and religion are rather empty. The only thing is living affection, and of that I have had the most touching experience. — You have your children and I envy your possession of them — not, of course, that

---

[27] Maitland, X. 187
[28] ibid., XVI. 352

I can imagine loving anyone better than my poor little Laura, but I should like to have more Lauras.»[29]

He was to get them. It so happened that the next house to his, 13, Hyde Park Gate South (since 1884, 22 Hyde Park Gate) was occupied by a widow, Mrs. Herbert Duckworth, with her three children (including Gerald, the future publisher of Virginia Woolf's first novel). The Duckworths and the Stephens had been very friendly. On January 9, 1878, Stephen writes to J. R. Lowell: »Mrs. Duckworth has passed through seven years of widowhood in retirement from the world and entire devotion to her children and her sick and troubled relations. I have always pitied her and revered her. She has been so noble, so patient and unselfish. No one can be surprised that after her unfailing goodness to me and mine I should have fallen in love with her.»[30] They were married in 1878. »If I am not happy again», Stephen wrote to O. W. Holmes, »it will be my own fault.»[31]

The first Mrs. Leslie Stephen with her round, dimpled face and engaging smile, had been a thoroughly womanly woman. The second was a mature, Madonna-like beauty. She had large heavy-lidded blue eyes, an oval face and a slender neck. Her figure was tall and slim. But behind that austerely pure Pre-Raphaelite appearance there flashed that impish glint of humour that we meet in her youngest daughter, Virginia. Perhaps it is, as her daughter assumes, the trace of French blood in her, that accounts for the sudden bubbling into merriment and delightful whimsicality that made Mrs. Stephen so fascinating and sought-after in company. She must have been the origin of Mrs. Ambrose in *The Voyage Out*, »who could dance for ever»[32] — even at the advanced age of forty! But she is also Mrs. Ramsay, »who would never for a single second regret her decision, evade difficulties or slur over duties».[33] »Julia used to be

---

[29] ibid., XIV. 286
[30] ibid., XV. 311
[31] ibid., XV. 310
[32] *The Voyage Out*. p. 187
[33] *To the Lighthouse*. p. 16

'at home' on Sunday afternoons», runs Leslie Stephen's description of his wife, »and though we did not attempt to set up a literary or artistic 'salon', I can see her surrounded on such occasions by a very lively and pleasant group. Especially, I may say, she took the keenest possible interest in young people: she was loved and admired in return by many young friends; she was happy in watching their friendships or love-makings, and her pleasure was in itself a refinement and a charm. Her courtesy was perfect — sometimes a tacit rebuke to me, who find courtesy to bores a very difficult duty.»[34] There we have the prototypes of Mr. Ramsay »slamming out of the room», and Mrs. Ramsay with »her extreme courtesy, like a Queen raising from the mud a beggar's dirty foot and washing it».[35]

Four children were born between 1879 and 1883: Vanessa, Thoby, Virginia, and Adrian. Mrs. Stephen had her hands full in the household where she had an extra child, and sometimes quite a difficult one, in her husband. Guests were entertained: Henry James, Thomas Hardy, John Ruskin, and Darwin came; George Meredith was one of the best friends of the family, so were George Eliot and her husband and R. L. Stevenson. Endless discussions of the learned men were to be suffered: »— — who had won this, who had won that, who was a 'first-rate man' at Latin verses, who was 'brilliant, but I think fundamentally unsound', who was undoubtedly the 'ablest fellow in Balliol', who had buried his light temporarily at Bristol or Bedford, but was bound to be heard of later when his Prolegomena — to some branch of mathematics or philosophy saw the light of the day.»[36] Or else the talk was »on cubes and square roots; that was what they were talking about now; on Voltaire and Madame de Staël; on the character of Napoleon; on the French system of land tenure; on Lord Rosebery; on Creevey's Memoirs: she let it uphold her and sustain her, this admirable fabric of the masculine intelligence, which ran up and down, crossed this way and that, like iron girders spanning

---

[34] Maitland, XV, 323
[35] *To the Lighthouse*, p. 16
[36] ibid., pp. 16—17

the swaying fabric, upholding the world, so that she could trust herself to it utterly, even shut her eyes, or flicker them for a moment, as a child staring up from its pillow winks at the myriad layers of leaves of a tree. Then she woke up. It was still being fabricated. William Bankes was praising the Waverley novels.»[37] The delicious irony of the daughter's description was shared by her mother, we are sure. In fact it is confirmed by Mrs. Stephen's own literary product, a book called *Notes from Sick Rooms*, published in 1883. »The origin of most things has been decided on, but the origin of crumbs in bed has never excited sufficient attention among the scientific world,»[38] a quotation from a sketch called *On Bed Crumbs* has a quality which reminds us at once of her daughter's *On Being Ill* or *On Not Knowing Greek* and many other sketches and essays as well as of numerous glimpses in her novels. There we have the origin of Virginia Woolf's »whimsical hyperbole, the half-amused detachment, the trick of remote and yet illuminating reference, and something of the wondering contemplative mind», as Dr. Holtby rightly points out,[39] and not in her father's clear reasonings. That Mrs. Stephen could have time for literary activities amongst the tumult of her household, proves what a talented and energetic woman she must have been.

It was a happy gathering of people, the Stephen household. The cildren grew up surrounded by love, by culture, and by taste. Their father used to read aloud to the cildren from the time they were old enough to understand anything. He took them through *Tom Brown's School Days*, *Treasure Island*, and the *Waverly Novels* (his own favourites). Then followed Carlyle's *French Revolution*, *Vanity Fair*, Jane Austen's novels, Shakespeare, and poetry: Wordsworth, Tennyson, Matthew Arnold whose poems father could quote at any length by heart. »At the end of a volume», writes one of the daughters, »my father always gravely asked our opinion as to its

---

[37] ibid., p. 164

[38] quoted in Holtby, p. 12. The original at the British Museum is unavailable, being one of those destroyed in the bombings during the war.

[39] idem

merits, and we were required to say which of the characters we liked best and why».[40] A good elementary school for a future critic! To Vanessa (now Vanessa Bell, the painter), Stephen passed on his skill in drawing. The children were not taught any religion; their minds were left open to form their own opinions. Mrs. Ambrose's words (in *The Voyage Out*) are probably echoes of the Stephen nursery. »'She (the nurse) is a good woman as they go, but she is determined to make my children pray. So far, owing to great care on my part, they think of God as a kind of walrus.' — 'Oh, surely, Helen, a little religion hurts nobody.' — 'I would rather my children told lies.'»[41] Virginia Woolf is not very kind to religious people in her books, but in her last novel, *Between the Acts*, her vehemence seems to have developed into greater leniency.

For thirteen years the family went down to St. Ives, »at the very toe-nail of England», in the summer. The children loved the place, and it has left permanent traces in literature through Virginia Woolf's preoccupation with the waves and the sea, dating back to those carefree days.

But again the thunderbolt struck: after a very short illness Mrs. Stephen died in May, 1895. Poor Leslie Stephen was again cast down by sorrow, wanting to die himself but for his children. He blamed himself, conscientious as he was, for having been difficult and for having caused her unnecessary pain. »I am, like my father, 'skinless', over-sensitive and nervously irritable», he writes to his children some days after his wife's death. »I am apt also to be a little absent in mind, absorbed in thoughts about my books or my writings, and occasionally paying very little attention to what is passing around me. — I am inclined, too, to be often silent. — At the time of my nervous depression in particular, I become fidgety and troublesome in a social point of view. I am, I think, one of the most easily bored of mankind. I cannot bear long sittings with dull people, and even when alone in my family I am sometimes as restless as a hyena.

---

[40] quoted in Maitland, XXI, 474
[41] *The Voyage Out*, p. 22

I remember — and certainly not without compunction — with certain guests of ours, how I used to plunge away into my back den and leave them, I fear, to bore Julia. All this comes back to me — trifles and things that are not quite trifles — and prevents me from saying, as I would so gladly have said, that I never gave her anxiety or caused her needless annoyance.»[42] As if the children needed to be told! They knew their Mr. Ramsay, their exasperating (Leslie Stephen's silences could be devastating and the day of settling household bills like an earthquake!), but lovable Mr. Ramsay.

Leslie Stephen was as severe a critic of his own books as of his own character. »I did not send *Hours in a Library*», he writes to C. E. Norton, July 28, 1874, »because — it is a very foolish reason — I am — do not mention it to any one — rather ashamed of it. I don't know why, but I have a suspicion that I am not a good critic, or perhaps it is merely a case of distorted vanity . . . Don't say anything about the book when you write again, or it will seem to me as though I had been fishing for a compliment.»[43]

Life went on, as it must. Stella, the eldest Duckworth daughter took on the nursing of the despondent family back to normal life. She was 26. Two years later she married, but died after only three months. Death plays a leading role almost in all Virginia Woolf's novels. We do not feel surprised after learning what a frequent visitor death was in her home. Before she was 25 she had lost her grandparents, paternal whom she could not remember, maternal whom she could, her mother, her stepsister Stella, her father, and her brother Thoby. She was growing up in the shadow of death, she, as delicate in health as her father had been as a child, and as 'skinless'.

Outwardly the years that followed were happy. The young Duckworths and Stephens were great friends, and social life was lively. Their father was reaping success and fame: he was made an Honorary Doctor of Oxford, as well as of Cambridge, Edinburgh and Harvard,

---

[42] Maitland, XX. 433—4
[43] ibid., XII. 243

and an Hon. Fellow of Trinity Hall. In 1902 he became Sir Leslie Stephen, K. C. B. — an honour which his modesty would have compelled him to refuse but for the pressure of his children. Since 1898 he had been almost completely deaf, and about 1902 an internal trouble appeared which was to kill him two years later. He took it calmly, as a matter of course. On June 12, 1902, he writes to Norton: »For a time I fancied that a speedy end was probable, and it gave me no trouble. I could die, it seems to me, to-morrow without being much excited about it. Why should I? I have had, as you know, a full share of such happiness as comes to very few and I should despise myself if I whined ... On the whole therefore I can at present take matters calmly, and I think that my chief duty almost is to leave a tolerable memory of myself to the children.»[44] And he did.

Because of her delicate health, Virginia never went to school or college. Greek, among other things, was taught to her at home, and she had a free access to any book in her father's well-stocked library where the eighteenth century was especially well represented. Virginia was exceptionally fortunate in having unlimited intellectual and religious freedom, not common in those days. That was her most valuable inheritance. The friends played their part, too, in forming her world: »Here were always visitors — uncles and aunts and cousins 'from India' — and others of the solitary and formidable class, whom she was enjoined by her parents to 'remember all your life'. By these means, and from hearing constant talk of great men and their works, her earliest conceptions of the world included an august circle of beings to whom she gave the names of Shakespeare, Milton, Wordsworth, Shelley, and so on. — They made a kind of boundary to her vision of life, and played a considerable part in determining her scale of good and bad in her small affairs.»[45] To be thus reared under the auspices of Plato, Voltaire and other epoch-making thinkers of all time, might well foster tolerance and intellectual integrity, especially in a daughter of a Leslie Stephen, born with

---

[44] ibid., XX, 470
[45] *Night and Day*, p. 33

leanings towards moral earnestness, courage and sincerity as well as with the spark of literary creation. In addition to these paternal gifts, her mother gave Virginia beauty, a whimsical sense of humour, capacity for keen enjoyment and a touch of irony. Both parents may have contributed to give her a great, almost excessive, sensibility which caused nervous strain, an unnaturally keen alertness to things and an inward unbalance, hidden under a formidable mask of reserve. Her inner being, self-conscious, always upon the alert, always ready for a struggle between the conflicting elements, was reflected in her outward appearance. Her presence was felt immediately she entered the room, tall, slim, narrow-faced, with a melancholy expression in her large eyes, which could, through the flash of a smile, become lit up, making the face look oddly different. Her portraits tell us that her eyes were deep in their sockets, her mouth small and sensitive, her nose of a beautiful shape, her face almost fleshless. Those who knew her say that there was something fierce and frightening about her, but at the same time something graceful, poetic — an impression that her photographs confirm. The words she uses of Orlando could be applied to her: »A million candles burnt in her without her being at the trouble of lighting a single one.»[46] But the burning wick gradually eats up the candle.

At twenty-two, in 1904, when, after the death of their father, the Stephen sisters and brothers moved to 46, Gordon Square, W. C. 1, Virginia was still inexperienced and gawky, but already every inch »the queen of London literary circles» in the making, a lady of »wit, detachment, learning and poetry».

---

[46] *Orlando*, p. 115

II

To Bloomsbury via Cambridge

Virginia Woolf never went »up» to Cambridge as a student: she only went with a chaperone to visit her two brothers at Trinity College. Instead, Cambridge came to her. It came to her, first, through her father, and then through her brothers and their friends, one of whom became her husband and another married her sister Vanessa. She could not escape Cambridge.

When Virginia visited her brothers, she looked around with eager eyes, an amused smile, and, perhaps, with a slight, though secret antagonism, for Cambridge did not take kindly to women. Its atmosphere was purely masculine. The typical intellectual undergraduate was for her a man who »sits hour after hour with his toes on the fender, talking about philosophy and God and his liver and his heart and the hearts of his friends. They're all broken. You can't expect him to be at his best in a ballroom. He wants a cosy, smoky, masculine place, where he can stretch his legs out, and only speak when he's got something to say. — So far as brains go I think it's true what he said the other day: they're the cleverest people in England. But — he wants some one to laugh at him.»[1] The picture is without doubt true to life, being that of Virginia's close friends, which did not prevent her from smiling at them. »She (Helen Ambrose) was thinking of the clever, honest, interesting young men she knew, — and wondering whether it was necessary that thought and scholarship should thus maltreat their bodies, and should thus elevate their minds to a very high tower from which the human race appeared to them like rats and mice squirming on the flat.»[2] Was

---
[1] *The Voyage Out*, p. 183
[2] ibid., p. 242

Lytton Strachey perhaps in the writer's mind when she drew the picture? The professors and dons did not escape her scrutiny either. »He (Edward Pargiter, a don) was shy. He was spare and thin. He looked as if his face had been carved and graved by a multitude of fine instruments; as if it had been left out on a frosty night and frozen over. — His movements were from habit, not from feeling. — He hadn't worried himself about politics and money —. There was something sealed up, stated, about him. Poetry and the past, was it? — A professor? A master? Somebody who had an attitude fixed on him, from which he could not relax any longer.»[3] The confirmed and blissful bachelorhood of so many Cambridge men also aroused Virginia's desire to smile at them. Mr. Pepper, in *The Voyage Out*, »had not married himself for the sufficient reason that he had never met a woman who commanded his respect. — His ideal was a woman who could read Greek, if not Persian, was irreproachably fair in the face, and able to understand the small things he let fall while undressing —.»[4] Virginia's brothers and friends bore her criticisms valiantly. After all, she was only a woman. She could not be expected to understand the real values in life or the masculine point of view. Besides, she was only seventeen when her brothers went up to the university.

In 1899 the names of Thoby Stephen, Leonard Woolf, Clive Bell, Lytton Strachey, and Sydney Saxon Turner were among those entered in the registers of Trinity College, Cambridge. That particular college seems to have had a remarkable and varied collection of eminent men as Fellows at that time — as, indeed, at most times. Science was represented by Prófessor J. J. (later Sir Joshua) Thomson and his New Zealand assistant, E. Rutherford (later Baron Rutherford of Nelson) who, basing their work on the Continental discoveries of x-rays and the radioactivity of uranium, were trying to isolate the electron and to develop the atomic theories. Arthur (later Sir Arthur) Eddington and A. N. Whitehead were building up their fame in

---

[3] *The Years*, p. 306
[4] *The Voyage Out*, p. 21

physics and mathematics. Bertrand Russell was making himself known as an interpreter of Pure Mathematics as related to Logic. Henry Sidgwick, F. W. H. Myers, J. McT. E. McTaggart, and G. E. Moore were exploring the secrets of philosophy in its various aspects. Sidgwick was an empiricist, Myers was mainly interested in physical research, McTaggart proceeded on Hegelian metaphysical lines, and Moore represented what is known as philosophical realism. Our young friends rallied round Moore.

Neville's Court in Trinity College came to play an important part as a haven in the mental odyssey of our friends, for both Russell and Moore had their rooms on the north side of the court. The informal meetings of the group usually took place there. The admittance to the »inner circle» was not limited to Trinity people. G. Lowes Dickinson, Fellow of King's, was intimate with them; so was his great friend Roger Fry, who had already left Cambridge and science to become a painter, but continued in close contact with his former friends, especially McTaggart and Lowes Dickinson. Later E. M. Forster and J. M. (later Lord) Keynes, as well as J. T. Sheppard (now Sir John, Provost of King's) and Desmond (Sir Desmond) MacCarthy joined them.

What was the attraction of those »cosy, smoky, masculine» rooms? The question is perhaps best answered by a short characterization of the people at whose feet the younger disciples were sitting and worshipping, for the secret of the attraction lay in the force of powerful personalities, even more than in what they preached. Both Oxford and Cambridge have always believed in the formative influence of »characters», which very often included eccentricity. The great King's College figure O. B., Oscar Browning, certainly was an oddity as well as a personality. McTaggart too came very near to being an eccentric.

Althought it was not McTaggart's philosophy that our friends took up, he is necessary as a background in our picture, for he was a close friend of Lowes Dickinson and Fry. At one time he exercised considerable influence on Russell, too, although later Russell departed from the metaphysical doctrines and went his own way. Besides,

McTaggart is a prophet of friendship which was considered to be one of the most valuable aspects of what is, by our friends, called »good life».

McTaggart started being a »character» at a very early age. When he was six, he is said to have stopped in the middle of his play »to think about God». While at school, at the age of fourteen, he had read all Spencer's works and had come to accept atheism and materialism as his creed. It was about that time that Roger Fry began to find this uncouth, rather strange school-mate of his very attractive and most stimulating company. He never ceased to be stimulated by this friend with whom he shared rooms in Cambridge. From materialism McTaggart developed into Hegelian idealism through his studies in metaphysics which was included in his Moral Science Tripos in which he took a First Class (1888). Metaphysics led him to a passionate appreciation of human intercourse. He is said to have possessed real genius for friendship which stretched over class divisions and differences of age. A young farmer in New Zealand[5] was a friend valued as highly as a Lord Rutherford or a Prof. Sidgwick. »It had been», he writes in New Zealand, »an absolutely perfect day. What with the moonlight, the Hegel and N. (a young farmer, his special friend there) I was very ecstatic and the happiness was so intense as to be painful. The thing I felt most was how one would give up everything for love».[6] Indeed, the three things he valued most and believed in were Love, Truth, and Immortality. God had no intrinsic value in his philosophy except as a possible name for a Divine Unity. Reality meant for him a perfect harmony of all souls; nothing but souls was real. They would pass through innumerable incarnations before they arrived in heaven, which was a state of complete comprehension of others, where no misunderstandings were possible. »I can't help thinking it probable», he writes, »that people who meet once will meet often on the way up. That they should meet at all seems to show

---

[5] where his mother had emigrated and he himself was a frequent visitor, his wife also being a New Zealander.
[6] G. L. Dickinson: *J. McT. E. McTaggart*, p. 42

that they must be connected with the same part of the pattern of things, and if so, they would probably often be working together». »Very fanciful, no doubt», he adds, »but more probable than thinking that it goes by chance, like grains in a heap, which is what one thinks in these scientific days, unless one thinks for oneself».[7] The thrust was, perhaps, aimed at some of his friends. Russell, for one, must have been all impishness and humorously wrinkled smiles when hearing such sentimental ideas, his metaphysical phase being over by that time. Moore, one imagines, killed the McTaggartian attempts to reach heaven by a devastating shrug of his shoulders. We are subordinated to nature and its victims, Russell believes. Mental phenomena seem to him to be bound up with material structure. Thus body and soul cannot be disparate. God and immortality must therefore also remain dreams. But Russell does not deny that there is an element of wisdom to be learned from the mystical way of feeling. He commends mysticism, not as a way of getting at the truth, but as an attitude to life. In his search for truth he is all for sense, reason, and analysis as contrasted with revelation or insight or intuition, whatever you choose to call it. McTaggart's belief in the mystical »beyondness» was strengthened by his own experience of what he called his »Saul-feeling», a mystical amalgamation with the Universe. As time went on, he became more and more convinced about the all-importance of Love, about its being the highest thing in the world. »If the love for one person», he says, »could be felt as what did sum up the whole Universe, that would be the culmination of all things».[8] McTaggart was by most people considered an eccentric. His friends found him »adorable» and his opponents »disgustingly sentimental». Yet, despite differences of opinion, there was something in his passionate appreciation of friendship that appealed even to those who were otherwise opposed to his ideas. There was, however, at least one kindred soul who agreed with McTaggart on most points: his future biographer Goldsworthy Lowes Dickinson.

---

[7] ibid., p. 37
[8] ibid., p. 95

Those two had been friends ever since their undergraduate days. Both had belonged since 1887 to the Apostles — a very select discussion society which had included Tennyson and Hallam in the eighteen twenties. In the same year Roger Fry also was elected, feeling »much awed by thus becoming a member of so distinguished and secret a society».[9] It was considered a much greater honour than winning a scholarship. The members met once a week to discuss »things in general», i.e. religion, philosophy, and politics.

For Lowes Dickinson, Plato and the Greek ideals were all-important, so important indeed that he made it his life's work to interpret them to his compatriots. This influence can be traced through the whole span of his mature life starting with the publication of *The Greek View of Life* (1895) and ending in the year of his death, 1932, with *The Contribution of Ancient Greece to Modern Life*. The titles of his other principal philosophical works, *The Meaning of Good* (1901), *A Modern Symposium* (1905), *After Two Thousand Years* (1930), and *Plato and his Dialogues* (1931) reveal the same theme. Even *The Magic Flute* (1920), though inspired by Mozart's opera, — Mozart and Goethe being his other great loves — preaches Greek philosophy. The figures are Mozart's, but their ideas are mainly Plato's. We meet Pamina, Tamino, and Papageno as mouthpieces of philosophical doctrines; Sarastro, the King, is a symbol of reason, the Queen of Night that of desires and emotions. In the Hall of Sarastro, where the worthies lead their everlasting life, we meet Ptolemy, Socrates, and Aristotle, among others, but Plato has fallen back under the domination of the Queen »because he had become to prefer religion to reason, authority to liberty, and the State to the individual».[10] Indeed, *The Magic Flute* could be called almost its writer's Credo, for all the fundamental values in life — religion, immortality, truth — are discussed on its pages, mostly in the Platonic form of dialogue. Religion for Lowes Dickinson means following Truth in Love. Immortality is reached by following Truth

---

[9] Virginia Woolf: *Roger Fry*, p. 50
[10] *The Magic Flute*, p. 118

for Truth's sake. Truth, again, is defined as meaning two things, »first, truth of fact, and, secondly, truth of value. — What is the evidence of truth of fact? — The perceptions of the outer senses, enlarged by instruments, corrected by comparison, and related by logic. — What is the evidence of truth of value? — The perception of the inner senses, tested and developed by experience. — Is there any other method of Truth? — There is none.»[11]

Lowes Dickinson shares with McTaggart a belief in there being a pattern of life. He thinks that »behind all this process we call history, chaotic though it seems, there is an urge driving men, reluctant and obstructive though they be, towards a purpose which is both their own and that of something greater than they; that a light is beginning fitfully to dawn upon their darkness; the light of knowledge and of truth».[12] He, like Russell at that time, believed in the right kind of education as a remedy for the state of the world. It has to be of two kinds, »the one capable of sufficient demonstration, which we call specifically science, that which attempts to determine the temporal order of events, and of which the principles can and should be taught to everyone; the other, concerned with values and purposes, about which there is more disagreement, and which, I think, cannot be taught, both dogmatically and truly by any religion or any philosophy, but should be gradually brought to light by free and open discussion, in which bad premises and bad conclusions should conflict with good, in the hope, or rather the faith, that sooner or later the latter will prevail».[13] The latter was the Socratic method he himself followed in most of his books: different opinions are brought up in the discussion; the reader has to draw his own conclusions as to the preferability of the expressed ideas. Yet on one point all our friends agreed, however much they may have differed on others, and that was on love coming nearer than any other form of our experience to being absolutely good.

---

[11] ibid., p. 125
[12] *After 2000 Years*, pp. 115 ff.
[13] ibid., pp. 116 ff.

Both McTaggart and Lowes Dickinson were thorough-bred idealists, dreamers, deemed by many almost naïve in their beliefs. The First World War nearly broke Lowes Dickinson's heart, but in McTaggart it brought to the surface his fanatical old-school-tie devotions (he had always been a staunch Tory, and »a Jingo» at that) and his love of everything British. He went so far as to become one of the most ardent advocates of the expulsion of his old friend Bertrand Russell from Cambridge because of the latter's anti-war activities in 1916. This attitude of McTaggart's separated him also from Lowes Dickinson, who remained faithful to his pacifist ideals, though he was never so provocative as Russell. He found consolation in his work for the League of Nations, the constitution of which was partly drafted by him in its early stages.

But the havoc the wars were to cause was still very far and quite impossible to imagine at the beginning of the century. It was firmly believed that the world was progressing and reason getting the upper hand both in the government of nations and the self-control of individuals. Life seemed altogether secure, and abstract ideas the only values worth considering. Beauty, truth, and love were the catchwords in the air of the Cambridge of that decade.

In 1903 three books of fundamental value in their respective branches of science were published by Trinity men: F. W. H. Myers's posthumous *Human Personality and its Survival of Bodily Death*, G. E. Moore's *Principia Ethica*, and Bertrand Russell's *Principles of Mathematics*. What a wealth of interchange of opinions there must have been at the high table of Trinity where such widely different fields of thought were represented! That Cambridge was a centre of psychical research as well as of pure logic, is a proof of its open-minded scientific spirit, although at that time psychical research was only grundgingly, if at all, admitted among the branches of science. Our friends were not enthusiastic. Even Lowes Dickinson, who, like McTaggart, became a member of the Society for Psychical Research, founded in 1887 under Prof. Henry Sidgwick's presidency, felt sceptical about the results. All the others emphatically shared Russell's opinion, when he said: »For my part, I consider the evidence so far adduced by psychical research in favour of survival much weaker than the physiological evidence on the other side. But I fully admit that it might at any moment become stronger, and in that case it would be unscientific to disbelieve in survival.»[14] E. M. Forster is — for him — surprisingly heated on this point calling psychical research »that dustbin of spirit».[15]

Metaphysics and psychical research were not for our young men. Instead, to be told that you could find out everything by pursuing methodical questioning and by aiming at verbal precision, was highly stimulating. Moore s »do we desire to desire to desire to desire»[16] sounded wonderfully precise in their ears. To think correctly was to arrive at the ultimate truths, Moore, and with him his disciples maintained. Thus the Hegelian-McTaggartian obscure speculations were nowhere at all in their estimation. Kant, and his Categorical Imperative, had to go too. »It is plain». Moore argues, »that what exists eternally cannot be affected by our actions; and only what is affected by our actions can have a bearing on their value as means; so *nothing ought to be done*».[17] But of far greater practical consequence was that also the Utilitarian creed had to go, though Moore admitted that the *practical* conclusions at which the Benthamites arrived were not far from the truth, although their *reason* for holding that pleasure alone is good as an end, was wrong. Through Keynes Moore's influence must have reached people and nations who have never even heard the philosopher's name. »We were amongst the first of our generation», writes Lord Keynes, »perhaps alone amongst our generation to escape from the Benthamite tradition», which he regards as »a worm which has been gnawing at the insides of modern civilisation and is responsible for its present moral decay».[18] Their liberalism in politics was also based on Moore's theories. Keynes defines their outlook as »an escape from Bentham, joined with the

---

[14] *What I Believe*, p. 16
[15] *Goldsworthy Lowes Dickinson*. p. 122
[16] *Principia Ethica*, I. 13. 16
[17] ibid., IV. 68. 117
[18] *Two Memoirs*. pp. 96 ff.

unsurpassable individualism of our philosophy, which has served to protect the whole lot of us from the final *reductio ad absurdum* of Benthamism known as Marxism. We have completely failed, indeed, to provide a substitute for these economic bogus-faiths capable of protecting or satisfying our successors. But we ourselves have remained — am I not right in saying *all* of us? — altogether immune from the virus, as safe in the citadel of our ultimate faith as the Pope of Rome in his».[19]

Their attitude was a mixture of aristocratic ideals, social conscience, and radical tendencies. McTaggart, for instance, despite his Toryism, was Liberal in many internal affairs, and even Radical in the matters concerning University. He voted for women's degrees and for the abolition of compulsory Greek. He also sided entirely with the other members of our group in their advocacy of women's suffrage, and of open discussion on sex and religion. It was mainly in foreign policy that he took a »Jingo» view. Lowes Dickinson was as romantic a Democrat as can be expected. By nature, he was an aristocrat, but his universal love of mankind in all its follies made him consider the happiness of the masses more important than the preservation of the so-called Higher Goods for an élite. He not only theorized, but went to work on a co-operative farm as a farm-hand. True, the experiment only lasted two months, but it proves his sincerity and good will. In *A Modern Symposium* the question of masses versus élite is discussed at greater length. Sir John Harrington, a gentleman of leisure, represents the élite and holds with Plato and Aristotle that the masses ought to be treated as means, as subordinates to a higher end, and that the good life must either be the privilege of a few, or not exist at all. There, Plato and his English disciple differed. Lowes Dickinson's loving heart could not think of anybody as a slave. All our friends shared Moore's passionate appreciation of freedom as something »without which, possibly, nothing very good can exist in this world».[20] although it may not be

---

[19] ibid., p. 97
[20] *Principia Ethica*, VI. III. 186

of any value in itself and by no means certain even to produce anything of value. In theory communism attracted them, but in its Russian form it was found unpleasant. Russell went to Russia in 1920 to see with his own eyes how things were there. He returned disillusioned, and has remained disillusioned ever since. Keynes too found the régime unsuitable for Western minds, when he visited Russia in 1925. But both of them retained their belief in the social conception of welfare covering the whole community. Russell, like Lowes Dickinson, discarded the aristocratic ideal that existed in Greece. »Certain good things», he says, »such as art and science and friendship, can flourish very well in an aristocratic society. They existed in Greece on the basis of slavery; they exist among ourselves on a basis of exploitation. But love, in the form of sympathy or benevolence, cannot exist freely in an aristocratic society. — The limitations of sympathy involved in the aristocratic ideal are its condemnation.»[21] On the same principle nationalism was also condemned by Russell as a limitation of sympathy to one's own compatriots. It was on this that he based his pacifism during the First World War which caused such antagonism against him, as indeed against many other members of the group. Russell was expelled from Cambridge, fined a hundred pounds which he refused to pay, and, in 1918, convicted for six months. Lytton Strachey was also brought before a tribunal as a conscientious objector. In the Second World War the wheel had come full circle: our friends had ceased to be conscientious objectors, and their children had gone even further. Clive and Vanessa Bell's talented son, Julian, had become greatly interested in military history, insisted on going to drive an ambulance in the Spanish War against the warnings and exhortations of his family and friends, and was killed there. In a BBC discussion on the atomic bomb on November 10, 1949, Bertrand Russell emphatically declared that if the circumstance arose when he would have to choose between war and Russian domination, he would unhesitatingly choose war.

But at the beginning of the century Russell was still of the

---

[21] *What I Believe*, pp. 69 ff.

opinion that wars were unnecessary and made-up things. Fear, he claimed, is at the back of men's »bad« desires, and the first task of the scientific moralist is to combat fear by increasing security, based on social justice, on the recognition of equal claims of all human beings, and by cultivating courage. Hence his opposition to all wars, his fight for the abolition of poverty, his advocacy of the League of Nations and of free speech in every field. Russell's ideas were eagerly accepted by all our friends except McTaggart, whose philosophy led him to consider poverty as a mere stepping stone to the Higher Life. Russell, like Lowes Dickinson, believed in education, in the early training of the faculties for what is called the good life: intelligence, self-control, and sympathy. »To live a good life in the fullest sense a man must have a good education, friends, love, children (if he desires them), a sufficient income to keep him from want and grave anxiety, good health, and work which is not uninteresting.«[22] When asked what good life is, Russell answers very much in the same words as Moore and Lowes Dickinson: that it is one inspired by love and guided by knowledge. Love at its purest combines indissolubly two elements: pure delight in contemplation on the one hand, and on the other, pure benevolence. Under the heading of the pure delights come the aesthetic enjoyments which, according to Moore, include »not merely a bare cognition of what is beautiful in the object, but also some kind of feeling or emotion. — All of these emotions are essential elements in great positive goods; they are *parts* of organic wholes, which have great intrinsic value«.[23] By far the most valuable things in life are considered certain states of consciousness roughly described as the pleasures of human intercourse and the enjoyment of beautiful objects. They are good in themselves, worth having purely for their own sakes, provided they are constituted of, what is termed by Moore, appropriate emotion, cognition of truly beautiful qualities, and true belief. The cognition of the beautiful qualities does not include any emotion, but is merely the consciousness of them.

---

[22] ibid., p. 68
[23] *Principia Ethica*, VI. 114. 189—190

To assert that a thing is beautiful is to assert »that the cognition of it is an essential element in one of the intrinsically valuable wholes; — the question, whether it is truly beautiful or not, depends upon the *objective* question whether the whole in question is or is not truly good, and does not depend upon the question whether it would or would not excite particular feelings in particular persons. — To say that a thing is beautiful is to say, not indeed that it is *itself* good, but that it is a necessary element in something which is: to prove a thing is truly beautiful is to prove that a whole, to which it bears a particular relation as a part, is truly good.»[24] The quotation is a good example of Moore's method and style, of its mathematical preciseness, which so fascinated his disciples. Moore discarded the Metaphysicians' idea of a supersensible reality. 'Good' is an ultimate, unanalysable predicate in the same way as 'true' is unanalysable. 'The good' is analysable, being = that which is good. Good as an end and good as a means must be kept strictly apart: »Whenever we judge that a thing is 'good as a means', we are making a jugment with regard to its causal relations: we judge *both* that it will have a particular kind of effect, *and* that that effect will be good.»[25] Moore's objection to Christian Ethics is based on this very fact that it does not distinguish whether its approval asserts 'This is a means to good' or 'This is good in itself'. The states of consciousness are for Moore the *raison d'être* of virtue; they form the rational ultimate end of human action and the sole criterion of social progress. There is thus no *intrinsic* value in virtue which Moore defines as »an habitual disposition to perform certain actions, which generally produce the best possible results».[26]

It was with a sense of exhilarating freedom that our friends entered the timeless realm of good states of mind shutting out the outer world with its actions and duties. »Our 'duty'», Moore declared, »is merely that which will be a means to the best possible, and the

---

[24] ibid., VI. 121. 201—2
[25] ibid.. I. 16. 22
[26] ibid.. V. 103. 172

expedient, if it is really expedient, must be just the same. We cannot distinguish them by saying that the former is something which we ought to do, whereas of the latter we cannot say we *'ought'*. In short, the two concepts are not, as is commonly assumed by all except Utilitarian moralists, simple concepts ultimately distinct. There is no such distinction in Ethics. The only fundamental distinction is between what is good in itself and what is good as a means, the latter of which implies the former.»[27] [28] Our young men were thrilled, and with a great sense of elation called themselves immoralists. »We recognised», writes Lord Keynes, »no moral obligation on us, no inner sanction, to conform or to obey. Before heaven we claimed to be our own judge in our own case».[29]

Our friends preached emancipation from all conventions: religion, family, and morals. Butler's *Way of All Flesh* was eagerly consulted. But where Butler had parental tyranny and filial hatred, our friends had mutual respect and affection. The sham they saw around them under the respectable surface of Victorian morals and religion did not apply to their own families, who were particularly sincere in their beliefs. The sons' fervour which found outlet through unorthodox channels was of the same substance as the missionary spirit that had inspired their families, in most cases for generations. They were idealists wanting to live in the world of truth, not of humbug and sham.

McTaggart's mother had been an Agnostic, and he himself, a true seeker, had passed through a course of development spanning two such distant poles as materialism and Hegelian idealism. As to Lowes Dickinson, his father, a portrait painter, had been a friend of Kingsley and F. D. Maurice, and was thus connected with Christian Socialism. His mother was also deeply religious. There was in the family a strong devotion to social services which in the son manifested itself in various ways, notably in his zeal for international co-opera-

---

[27] *Principia Ethica*, V. 101. 167

[28] cf. I. A. Richards on the subject in his *Principles of Lit. Crit.*, e.g. p. 23, p. 38.

[29] *Two Memoirs*, p. 98

tion. In religion he departed from the family tradition and approached, like most of his friends, what Keynes terms as neoplatonism.[30] Roger Fry's parents, Sir Edward and Mariabella Fry, both came from old Quaker families. At least eight generations of them had declined to take the oath in any form despite the fact that many professions were thus barred to them. In the seventeenth century one of their ancestors had been sentenced to three months' imprisonment for refusing to take the oath of allegiance. Their religion made them consider all art sinful. Drawing and water colours were tolerated, but it must have been a great sorrow to the parents that their son decided to leave his promising career as a scientist to take up painting. Their relations, however, remained cordial. G. E. Moore's father had been a doctor; so, too, his grandfather who had, besides, tried his hand at writing -semi-philosophical books. His mother came from a well-known Quaker family, the Sturges, but the Moores were Baptists. The son went through a religious phase at as early an age as ten or twelve when he became a Jesus-lover and even tried to convert other people. Under the influence of his elder brother, then an art student, he later became an Agnostic.

The family traditions were alive in all our friends, but in no one more than Bertrand Russell with all his unorthodoxy. His parents, Lord and Lady Amberley, had died when Bertrand was quite small. They had both been free-thinkers as well as Utilitarians and advocates of such advanced ideas as women's suffrage and birth control. Because of his opinions, Lord Amberley was vilified by his political opponents. He was, for instance, in a cartoon called 'Vice-count Amberley'. His son, basing his judgment on his father's letters and memoirs which he collected and published, describes him as »shy, studious and ultra-conscientious — perhaps a prig, but the very opposite of a rake».[31] It is psychologically a most interesting fact that, although Bertrand Russell only learnt to know his father's

---

[30] ibid., p. 186

[31] *My Mental Development* in *The Library of Living Philosophers*, ed. by Paul Arthur Schilpp, vol. V, p. 4

mind at the age of twenty, his own mental development had already been very much the same. And that although he was brought up in the house of his grandfather, Earl Russell, almost entirely cut off from the influence of the outer world, except through books. Lord Amberley had appointed two free-thinkers as his son's guardians, but Earl Russell persuaded the Court of Chancery to set aside the will. Thus Bertrand came to grow up under the strict guidance of his grandfather, or rather his grandmother, for Earl Russell died in 1878. She was as great a personality as her husband, coming from a family of Scots Presbyterians. Her views on right and wrong were rigid, and she had a firm belief in the individual conscience. At the age of seventy she became a Unitarian and an advocate of Home Rule for Ireland as well as a fierce opponent of Imperialism. »Thou shalt not follow a multitude to do evil», was a maxim she chose to be written on the fly-leaf of the Bible she gave to her grandson on his twelfth birthday. And another: »Be strong, and of good courage; be not afraid, neither be thou dismayed; for the Lord Thy God is with thee withersoever thou goest.» These maxims are as much a key to the character of the receiver as of the giver. A trait of fierce individualism and of integrity of conscience has been a characteristic of the family for generations. Bertrand fits well into the line that started with the rebellious Russell who was executed under the reign of Charles II.

By the time Bertrand entered Trinity College in 1890, he had already become acquainted with Mill's theories. Mill's influence was ousted by McTaggart's idealism to which Russell became converted in 1894. Prof. Henry Sidgwick, too, was one of his teachers, but as he represented the British empiricism, Russell did not at that time value him as highly as later. In 1898 G. E. Moore delivered his series of lectures on Leibniz. As a result out went Plato, Hegel, and Kant with their idealism. In came Leibniz, Locke, Hume, and, above everybody else, G. E. Moore: empiricism and realism.

But of as great an importance as any theories and doctrines, philosophic or otherwise, was the fact that Cambridge opened for Russell a »world of infinite delight», as he himself says, that of friendship which he had so far lacked entirely. He had felt lonely and unhappy until he went to Trinity where he found a group of friends, »able young men» who had not yet adopted the pose of cynical superiority which came in some years later and was first made fashionable in Cambridge by Lytton Strachey. »The world seemed hopeful and solid; we all felt convinced that nineteenth-century progress would continue, and that we ourselves should be able to contribute something of value. For those who have been young since 1914 it must be difficult to imagine the happiness of those days», he writes.[32]

The problem of perfect personal relationships had always occupied cultivated Western minds ever since the Greek philosophers. »The utmost giving of oneself to another up to the utmost limit of his power of receiving» is, according to Duns Scotus, »the most perfect moral virtue and the most perfect justice». There was a strong tradition in Cambridge, too, thanks to such prophets of friendship as McTaggart and Lowes Dickinson. To the former, with all his love of conviviality and his mystical interpretation of friendship, the evenings spent among kindred souls were an ante-room to heaven. »One used to come away afterwards late at night», he writes, »and stroll down the moonlit Backs of King's with a feeling as though an apocalypse had opened».[33] Moore, too, for all his intellectualism, discovered that forming intimate links with clever people for the first time in his life proved a fruitful inspiration. »Until I went to Cambridge», he says, »I had no idea how exciting life could be».[34] But no one has expressed it with greater charm and poetry than E. M. Forster recapturing his own feelings as well as those of his friend Lowes Dickinson in whose *Life* he has woven the following passage: »As Cambridge filled up with friends it acquired a magic quality. Body and spirit, reason and emotion, work and play, architecture and scenery, laughter and seriousness, life and art —

---

[32] ibid., p. 9
[33] Goldsworthy Lowes Dickinson: *J. McT. E. McTaggart*, p. 21
[34] *The Library of Living Philosophers*, ed. by Paul Arthur Schilpp, vol. IV, p. 12

these pairs which are elsewhere contrasted were there fused into one. People and books reinforced one another, intelligence joined hands with affection, speculation became a passion, and discussion was made profound by love.»[35] Indeed, you have only to walk to King's Bridge and see the proportionate architectural beauty of Clare, the magnificent contours of King's Chapel, and the grave dignity of Gibbs' Building to have a vision of centuries of culture and wealth. To see Nature in its glory you have only to look left to add to the picture the weeping willows drooping over the peaceful Cam, partly screening the walls and spires of St. John's. You have only to wander through the Backs on a mild summer evening listening to the nightingales to catch the harmony of poetry and nature. The eternal values are there almost within the reach of your hand.

The British culture of the nineteen-twenties was in many of its best manifestations permeated with the heritage of Cambridge. *The Longest Journey* by E. M. Forster is through and through a Cambridge book where the ideas that our group of young men had absorbed in their undergraduate days are reflected. In Virginia Woolf's *The Voyage Out, Jacob's Room*, and *The Waves* the essence and many of the actual conversations are Cambridge. Russell's and Keynes's illusion of the rationality of human nature echoes Moore's teachings. Clive Bell's *Civilization* is a mixture of the elements he has got mainly from Plato, Lowes Dickinson, Russell, and Moore, with an Epicureanism of his own. Lytton Strachey's devastating wit and his tendency to see human beings, as Virginia Woolf put it, »like rats and mice squirming on the flat», were partly derived from the school of Butler, Gosse, Russell, and Moore. Sir Desmond MacCarthy was an unmistakable, though 'humanized' variation of the intellectual school of our prophets. The politico-economic theories of Leonard Woolf were imbibed at the fountain where Keynes stilled his thirst. And so on. The student of British culture, like Virginia Woolf, cannot escape Cambridge.

---

[35] E. M. Forster: *G. Lowes Dickinson,* p. 35

III

The Atmosphere of Bloomsbury

In the spring of 1949, a small book called *Olivia*, written by »Olivia»,[1] was published and hailed by the best critics in England as a small masterpiece and as a specially 'Bloomsbury' book. The common reader may have felt slightly puzzled by the epithet, which was obviously used by way of praise.

For an ordinary Londoner, Bloomsbury is simply a quarter in London, limited on the south side by New Oxford Street, and on the other sides approximately by Tottenham Court Road, Gray's Inn Road, and Euston Road. For a visitor to London it mainly means the whereabouts of the British Museum which occupies a large block within the area, next door to London University buildings. For anyone familiar with modern English literature, the name has, however, a definite connotation. For him, Bloomsbury was the centre of a literary coterie whose fame was at its highest in the twenties. It is a name which in literary circles used to be — and still is — uttered with irony or with reverence, but very seldom with indifference.

When Frank Swinnerton, a fierce critic of the set, called Bloomsbury, with an ironic undertone, »the spiritual home of exiles from Cambridge University»,[2] he was perfectly right. There is a marriage between Cambridge and Bloomsbury. Our friends, »the exiles», now more or less settled in their walks of life, found asylum at 46, Gordon Square, in Bloomsbury, where the Stephen children had moved after the death of their father, Sir Leslie, in 1904. It remained

---
[1] Dorothy Strachey Bussy
[2] *The Georgian Lit. Scene*, p. 251

their home for three years, till 1907, when Vanessa married Clive Bell. Adrian and Virginia Stephen (Thoby had died suddenly after travelling in Greece in 1905) then moved to 29, Fitzroy Square, later to Brunswick Square. In 1912 Virginia married Leonard Woolf. In 1924 the Woolfs settled down at 52, Tavistock Square and then at 37, Mecklenburgh Square, so that Bloomsbury still continued to be the meeting-place. The Bells and the Frys lived in the vicinity, and the rest of their friends flocked into Bloomsbury in the evenings, at one or another of their friends' homes to enjoy what was meat and drink to them: talk. It was a continuation of the intimate gatherings of the so-called Midnight Society in the rooms of Cambridge colleges.[3] »Talking, talking, talking — as if everything could be talked — the soul itself slipped through the lips in thin silver disks which dissolve in young men's minds like silver, like moonlight. Oh, far away they'd remember it, and deep in dulness gaze back on it, and come to refresh themselves again.«[4] That happened usually on Thursday evenings, when whisky, buns, and cocoa were served for friends who could drop in at any time during the evening, even very late, for it was seldom that the company parted before two or three in the morning.[5] Virginia, who was later to record the spirit of these happy meetings very faithfully in her novels, was in the beginning a very shy young lady, almost fiercely self-conscious. At first she remained a mere listener, faithful, but not always very reverent. She would have her caustic smile sometimes when she listened to the young men who did their best to pull the world to pieces. »Youth, youth, — something savage — something pedantic. For example, there is Mr. Masefield, there is Mr. Bennett. Stuff them into the flame of Marlowe and burn them to cinders. Let not a shred remain. Don't palter with the second-rate. Detest your own age. Build a better one. And to set that on foot read incredibly dull essays upon Marlowe to your friends. For which purpose one must collate editions

---

[3] Cf. Annan: *Leslie Stephen*, p. 123

[4] Virginia Woolf: *Jacob's Room*, p. 39

[5] Cf. Duncan Grant's description of the evenings in *Horizon* June 1941, vol. III, No. 18, pp. 402 ff.

in the British Museum. One must do the thing oneself. Useless to
trust to the Victorians, who disembowel, or to the living, who are
mere publicists. The flesh and blood of the future depends entirely
upon six young men.»[6] The six young men she refers to might be,
let us say, Lytton Strachey, E. M. Forster, Maynard Keynes, Clive
Bell, Leonard Woolf, and Desmond MacCarthy. Talk flowed freely,
unguardedly, and candidly on any subject that came into their
minds. That was part of their gospel. But sooner or later it turned to
»something sensible», which to them meant the Greeks. »— yes, that
was what they talked about — how when all's said and done, when
one's rinsed one's mouth with every literature in the world, including
Chinese and Russian (but these Slavs aren't civilized), it's the flavour
of Greek that remains. Durrant quoted Aeschylus — Jacob Sophocles.
It is true that no Greek could have understood or professor refrained
from pointing out — Never mind; what is Greek for if not to be
shouted on Haverstock Hill in the dawn? Moreover, Durrant never
listened to Sophocles, nor Jacob to Aeschylus. They were boastful,
triumphant; it seemed to both that they had read every book in the
world; known every sin, passion, and joy. Civilizations stood round
them like flowers ready for picking. Ages lapped at their feet like
waves fit for sailing. And surveying all this, looming through the
fog, the lamplight, the shades of London, the two young men decided
in favour of Greece. 'Probably', said Jacob, 'we are the only people
in the world who know what the Greeks meant'. — A strange thing
— when you come to think of it — this love of Greek, flourishing
in such obscurity, distorted, discouraged, yet leaping out, all of
a sudden, especially on leaving crowded rooms, or after a surfeit
of print, or when the moon floats among the waves of the hills, or
in hollow, sallow, fruitless London days, like a specific; a clean blade;
always a miracle. Jacob knew no more Greek than served him to
stumble through a play. Of ancient history he knew nothing. However, as he tramped into London it seemed to him that they were
making the flagstones ring on the road to the Acropolis, and that
if Socrates saw them coming he would bestir himself and say 'my

[6] *Jacob's Room*, pp. 105—106.

fine fellows', for the whole sentiment of Athens was entirely after his heart; free, venturesome, high-spirited . . .»[7]

Round them, too, »civilizations stood like flowers ready for picking», and the conversation often took a natural turn from the Greeks to civilization on the whole and to the problems pertaining to it. They felt a great responsibility as promoters of culture. It was therefore most important to know exactly what was meant by the word. The main characteristics were agreed upon; they were »dominance of reason, intelligence, and knowledge over instinct, habit, and superstition»,[8] to use the words of Leonard Woolf, who, like all his friends, gives the highest place to Athens. He is ready to consider the Roman Empire as well, the Italy and England of the Renaissance, eighteenth-century France, and nineteenth-century England as the nearest approaches to real civilization. Clive Bell, who made civilization the theme of a closer study, is stricter and grants the highest place only to the three of them: Athens from the battle of Marathon to the death of Aristotle (480—322 B.C.), Renaissance Italy, from the death of Boccaccio in 1375 to the plunder of Rome in 1527, and France from the Fronde to the Revolution, between 1660—1789.

Clive Bell's *Civilization*, published in 1928, had been maturing in the author's mind ever since the earliest Bloomsbury days, according to his own statement in the dedication to Virginia Woolf, whom he thanks as his main help. As the book is an outcome of the spirit that inspired the group of friends who gathered to discuss things in what was the nearest approach to a literary salon in London in this century, it is important as a key to what is called the Bloomsbury atmosphere, although Clive Bell is a more exuberant, Epicurean exponent than most of the others. The more serious-minded, Leonard Woolf and Maynard Keynes for instance, would not like to be considered advocates for all that Clive Bell stood for.

Civilization follows in the steps of the Cambridge prophets, but

---

[7] ibid., pp. 74—75
[8] *Quack, Quack*, p. 17

in a mood that reminds one of a hilarious calf, kicking its legs for
sheer joy of life on its first outing in spring. The Hellenic atmosphere
is the intoxicating spring air, the Renaissance and the eighteenth-
century exuberance the fresh velvety breezes that drive away the
English winter fog and clear up the skies. Clive Bell is a rebel, but,
he says, everyone who wants to be civilized in England has to be
a rebel — a statement which sounds provocatively exaggerated, but
carries a great deal of truth. English society is to him — as it is
to E. M. Forster — an abomination. All he sees is a long vista of
»intellectual slums and garden suburbs». »An English boy», he says,
»born with fine sensibility, a peculiar feeling for art, or an absolutely
first-rate intelligence, finds himself from the outset at loggerheads
with the world in which he is to live. For him there can be no question
of accepting those national conventions which express what is
meanest in a distasteful society. To begin with, he will not go to
church or chapel on Sundays: it might be different were it a question
of going to Mass. The hearty conventions of family life which make
almost impossible relations at all intimate or subtle arouse in him
nothing but a longing for escape. He will be reared, probably, in an
atmosphere where all thought that leads to no practical end is
despised, or gets, at most, a perfunctory compliment when some
great man, who in the teeth of opposition has won to a European
reputation, is duly rewarded with a title or an obituary column in
The Times. As for artists, they, unless they happen to have achieved
commercial success or canonization in some public gallery, are pretty
sure to be family jokes. Thus, all his finer feelings will be constantly
outraged; and he will live a truculent, shamefaced misfit, with *John
Bull* under his nose and *Punch* round the corner, till, at some public
school, a course of compulsory games and the Arnold tradition either
breaks his spirit or makes him a rebel for life.»[9] — The Public School
has been condemned by numerous eminent men in their memoirs,
but when their turn has come to send their sons to school, as often
as not the Old School Tie has won. The Bells, however, remained

---

[9] *Civilization*, p. 57

faithful to their principles: their sons went to a progressive private school. — This sense of rebellion that Bell thinks to detect in finer spirits also goes to explain the fact that in England the best exponents of civilization are so often eccentrics, »characters», who want to assert their individuality even in their outward habits and appearance. »English civilization, or what passes for civilization», Clive Bell goes on with his condemnation, »is so smug and hypocritical, so grossly Philistine, and at bottom so brutal, that every first-rate Englishman necessarily becomes an outlaw. He grows by kicking».[10] The result is not, however, wholly negative, for although England is not »a pleasant country to live in for anyone who has a sense of beauty or humour, a taste for social amenities, and a thin skin», it breeds »that magnificently unmitigated individualism and independence which have enabled particular Englishmen of genius to create the greatest literature in all history and elaborate the most original, profound and fearless thought in modern».[11] An enthusiastic, but true statement. Hardly anyone would deny the abundance of individuality and orginality in the best British minds — Bloomsbury included.

In discussing what exactly civilization is, Clive Bell falls back upon the well-cherished doctrines of good states of mind that he and his friends so thoroughly discussed in their Cambridge days. Civilization, to put it shortly, is simply a means to good states of mind; not the only one, though, for there is a hierarchy in that realm, too. »Life, sun, rain, bread, wine, beauty, science and civilization», says Mr. Bell, »are all means to good; and the thing to bear in mind is, that while beauty is a direct means to good, and civilization a mediate, sun, rain, and life are remote, though essential, means».[12] In trying to outline the characteristics of civilized life, Clive Bell first eliminates those that are not necessary, though often counted among them. There he begins to tread controversial ground

---

[10] ibid., p. 58
[11] idem
[12] ibid., p. 13

by mentioning a sense of property, candour, cleanliness, belief in God, the future life and eternal justice, chivalry, chastity, patriotism, comfort, and creativeness. He admits that they may sometimes be means to good states of mind, but, in his provocative manner, points out that as often as not their necessity is only a pious wish. »In suitable hands, and at the right moment, gin and the Bible are means to good undoubtedly; yet it is a question how far European traders and missionaries are justified in calling what they carry into savage countries civilization.»[13]

When the author takes up defining the great periods of civilization in history, his opinions are not only interesting as such, but also revealing as an interpretation of what Bloomsbury aimed at being. It is, for instance, interesting to note his reasons for discarding the Romans from among what he calls The Paragons. The Romans cannot be counted among them, he says, for the surprising reason that »they were incapable of passionate love, profound aesthetic emotion, subtle thought, charming conversation, or attractive vices»,[14] all points in which Bloomsbury strove to excel. What he means is perhaps that the Romans were not sophisticated enough to be called really highly civilized, not artificial enough. The point is controversial, however, and not likely to be accepted without argument to the contrary. Be it as it may, the main characteristic of civilization is that it is something artificial. At its best we find it where a sense of values prevails and reason has become enthroned. The indisputably best example is given in Plato's Symposium where we get »a glimpse, and something more, of a civilization which seems to come nearer the heart's desire than anything less favoured ages have conceived possible».[15] How did it happen that the Greeks attained that high stage of development? It was due to the fact, says Clive Bell, that they had slaves who freed the citizens from menial work so that they could concentrate on other things, worthier

---

[13] ibid., p. 23
[14] ibid., p. 33
[15] ibid., p. 94

things, the things of the mind. To be completely civilized, a man must be free from material cares, is a recurrent theme in Bloomsbury books. We find it in Virginia Woolf as well as in E. M. Forster and the others. In the modern world the Athenian slaves have their equivalents in all those who live to produce rather than to enjoy. Inferiors they are only — for Bloomsbury takes a pride in thinking in democratic terms — in so far as they are incapable of thinking freely and feeling finely. Materially they may even be in a better position than the man of culture whose aim is not to be rich, but to live richly. That means cultivating his powers of thinking and feeling, pursuing truth and acquiring knowledge, not for any practical value that these may possess, but for themselves — »for their power of revealing the rich and complex possibilities of life».[16]

That leads us to the familiar question of ends and means and, further, to individualism which was the hallmark of the Athenians and equally greatly treasured by their Bloomsbury disciples. »Anyone who realizes that the sole good as an end is a good state of mind and that there are no grounds for supposing that such a thing as a collective mind exists, will naturally set store by the individual in whom alone absolute good is to be found»,[17] is a doctrine enthusiastically shared by all of them.[18] Individualism, again, results in Cosmopolitanism, »a movement of liberation from the herd instinct»,[19] as Clive Bell terms it, giving it a high place among the characteristics of civility. »A civilized man», he says, »sympathizes with other civilized men no matter where they are born or to what race they belong and feels uneasy with brutes and Philistines though they be

---

[16] ibid., p. 65

[17] ibid., p. 67

[18] Cf., for instance, E. M. Forster, *What I Believe*, p. 21. Bloomsbury helped to create the cult of individualism and the individual, well-suited for the rebellious and disillusioned twenties which thus became »the golden age» of Bloomsbury. Cf. Cyril Connolly, *Enemies of Promise*, p. 71; cf. also Noel Annan, *The Legacy of the Twenties*, The Listener, March 22, 1951, pp. 465 ff.

[19] *Civilization*, p. 67

his blood-relations living in the same parish».[20] Patriotism is, accordingly, not necessarily a virtue; on the contrary, it is very seldom that. The Athenians were admittedly very patriotic, but they have the excuse of having loved Athens for what she was and not just because she was *their* city. Also they had another excuse: their state was surrounded by hostile and menacing states which meant that thay had to be on the defensive all the time. Their patriotism was »intelligent and unsentimental»[21] and as such justifiable. Otherwise, if patriotism deteriorates into nationalism, it is a dangerous enemy to civilization. During the First World War Bloomsbury was, accordingly, pacifist.

The basic twin qualities in Greek life were »Reason, sweetened by a Sense of Values» and »a Sense of Values, hardened and pointed by Reason».[22] Of the later periods, the eighteenth century devoted itself to the cultivation of reason which endeared that period especially to Bloomsbury who accounted any kind of barbarism to people not using their reason. (But they never thought, as has often erroneously been claimed, that the world was, or people are, reasonable; people *should* be reasonable was what they meant.) The first characteristic which results from the enthronement of reason is tolerance which Bloomsbury considered one of the highest virtues of a civilized man. It makes us see that what we believe is not necessarily true, what we like not necessarily good, and that all questions are open. Voltaire's ideas exhilarated them. They joined him heartily in shouting »écrasez l'infâme», for they, too, considered the church a stronghold of superstition. But, they held, all prejudices are basically superstitions, mere taboos. Hence the mind must be free to wander and to touch anything under heaven. »Civilized people», Clive Bell says, »can talk about everything. For them no subject will be taboo so long as there is anything to say about it which seems interesting or gay».[23] In those matters mankind has progressed

---

[20] ibid., p. 69
[21] L. Woolf: *Quack, Quack*, p. 33
[22] *Civilization*, p. 45
[23] ibid., p. 90

— if progress it be — since Clive Bell wrote his book. But it has not resulted, as he rather presumes it would, in what he goes on to say next. The civilized man, he says, »must be free from prudery, superstition, false shame, and the sense of sin. This reason alone can do for him: and his moral code must repose on that other pillar of civility — a sense of values. His sense of values will tell him that the pleasures offered by the senses, or by an alliance between sense and intellect, are not bad in themselves. It will tell him, rather, that pleasure, so far as it goes, is always good: it is for civilized intelligence never to allow it to become a means to bad by hampering and making impossible greater good».[24] The, what Clive Bell calls »adorable»,[25] eighteenth century with its »sweet reasonableness»[26] had all those qualities which were so sadly lacking in the Victorian period, as Bloomsbury saw it. They bore a heavy grudge against it. But, then the preceding period seems nearly always to be lacking in attraction, whereas the one immediately before it possesses qualities that make us nostalgic. We have only to think of the numerous revaluations of the Victorian figures recently either published or broadcast in England to see that Lytton Strachey's portraits of them are beginning to be — probably only temporarily — out of fashion. The Victorian period — even its bourgeois civilization — begins to exercise fascination for the generation who has outlived the hardships and trials of the first half of the twentieth century. We turn our eyes longingly to the prosperity and peace of the previous century, whereas Bloomsbury, in the 'twenties, found fascinating the famous *salons* of Madame du Deffand, Mademoiselle Lespinasse and the others which were of such importance in eighteenth-century Paris. In these Parisian *salons* Bloomsbury found practically everything that makes life worth living: »a taste for truth and beauty, tolerance, intellectual honesty, fastidiousness, a sense of humour, good manners, curiosity, a dislike of vulgarity, brutality, and over-emphasis,

---

[24] idem
[25] ibid., p. 92
[26] Lytton Strachey, *Biographical Essays*, p. 201

freedom from superstition and prudery, a fearless acceptance of the good things of life, a desire for complete self-expression and for liberal education, a contempt for utilitarianism and philistinism, in two words — sweetness and light».[27] Here we have the ingredients of a civilized life, the Bloomsbury programme, if there was any definite programme. But the result, such as Clive Bell saw it, is not likely to be accepted by all as a true representative of the species, for Bell excludes every kind of extremist: the good man as well as the natural man, the artist, the hero, the saint, the philosopher, and the specialist, who, if pure types, do not fit within the bounds of an *uomo universale*. Few would presumably agree with him there. What is left could rather be stamped sophisticated than civilized, an Epicuranean whose main characteristics are that he appreciates art, respects truth, and knows how to behave himself. »To enjoy life to the full is his end, to enjoy it as a whole and in its subtlest and most recondite details; and to this end his chief means are the powers of thinking and feeling, intensely cultivated. He is a man of taste in all things. His intellectual curiosity is boundless, fearless, and disinterested. He is tolerant, liberal, and unshockable; and if not always affable and urbane, at least never truculent, suspicious, or overbearing. He chooses his pleasures deliberately, and his choice is limited neither by prejudice nor fear. Because he can distinguish between ends and means he values things for their emotional significance rather than their practical utility. All cant about 'rights', 'duties', and 'sanctities' blows past him like grit and chaff, annoying without injuring. His sense of values, intelligently handled, is a needle to prick the frothy bubbles of moral indignation. He is critical, self-conscious and, to some extent at any rate, analytical. Inevitably he will be egregious. Conscious of himself as an individual, he will have little sympathy with the unanimities of the flock: but educating his mind, his emotions and his senses, he will elaborate a way of life which he will clear, so far as possible, of obstructive

---

[27] *Civilization*, p. 104

habits and passions.»[28] This »amateur of exquisite states of mind»,[29] as Clive Bell aptly calls his — but not necessarily most people's — model specimen of a highly civilized person, can only flourish in material security; hence these exquisite states of mind must of necessity remain the privilege of the leisured classes, which leads us back to the idealization of the Athenian structure of society. This attitude — as mentioned before — is shared by all Bloomsbury and illustrated abundantly by Virginia Woolf, E. M. Forster, and others. Clive Bell is aware, however, that it may not please even all the members of the privileged classes, many of whom have the idiosyncrasy of considering equality a desirable thing. But, if so, Clive Bell points out, one must not then pretend to be an advocate of civilization; »equality, not good, is what you want. Complete human equality is compatible only with complete savagery».[30]

The position of women raises another controversial point. In Athenian society they, too, were divided into the leisured class and the slaves: the *hetairae* and the housewives. The latter did the work and bore the children, while the former sat at the festive tables of the members of the Symposiums taking part in the conversations. They were »the most brilliant, accomplished and learned ladies in Greece»,[31] and as a matter of course mistresses of their men friends. »The Athenians were not likely to forget that the most exquisite of human relations is the *liaison*, that the subtlest and most impalpable things of the spirit float from one mind to another most easily on a mixed flood of sense and emotion.»[32] Bloomsbury, a punster has tersely defined it, was place where »all the couples were triangles and lived in squares»![33] In Bloomsbury, as in Greece, the kind of

---

[28] ibid., pp. 118—119
[29] ibid., p. 124
[30] ibid., p. 127
[31] ibid., p. 145
[32] idem
[33] quoted in the *New Statesman and Nation*, March 29, 1941, Vol. XXI. No. 527, pp. 317—18

love felt by Sappho or Theognis was as well considered an acceptable form of personal relationship.

What Clive Bell is clearly after in his search for civilization is an enlightened democracy with an intellectual aristocracy — aristocracy carrying the meaning that E. M. Forster gave it: »the sensitive, the considerate, the plucky».[34] There must be liberty and justice in Bell's Utopia, but civilization must be left to an élite to propagate, supported by the government in the same way as it supports schools and universities. The members of the élite are to be elected at a fairly early age from among the most intelligent youth independent of what class they come from. Everyone ought to be given a good liberal education, but the education of the élite should be more elaborate. They should have all the means to culture and enough money to live comfortably; their fortunes ought not, however, to be allowed to increase. But it is only as a group that the élite can have a civilizing effect on others. It is the task of a »civilized nucleus» to radiate culture. »Only», Clive Bell points out, »when a number of civilized human beings come together does the civilized man become civilizing».[35] [36]

Was the gospel of the »civilized nucleus» in Bloomsbury, in the form Clive Bell preached it, accepted byt others as something worth spreading? When Bell's book was published it was attacked by the critics with glee. Around 1928 the Bloomsbury set was at the peak of its fame, and its influence unescapable. As they were a self-elected élite, the antagonism was, naturally, great. That the critics should have attacked the controversial points in which the book abounded, was as well only natural. Provocation was, partly, Clive Bell's aim, for anything is better than indifference in view of the importance of the theme. But that was just what some of the critics disapproved of. They thought Clive Bell's frivolous exuberance unsuitable for the treatment of so serious an argument. *The Times*

---

[34] *What I Believe*, p. 5

[35] *Civilization*, p. 119

[36] Cf. T. S. Eliot on the élite in his *Notes towards the Definition of Culture*, pp. 35 ff.

Literary Supplement speaks of the writer's »free exercise of his irresponsible intellect»[37] and bluntly calls his ideal life a life of dissipation. »For enjoyment the surfaces of things are enough, but life demands thickness and solidarity; that is where religion and morality come in — tedious matters to Mr. Bell, but to English people in general both still deeply evocative.»[38] The critics — with justification — wonder also whether the detachment and disinterestedness on which Bell and his friends pride themselves, may perhaps have severed them from the deeper sources of vital experience. »Here verse and thought and love are free; Great God! Give me captivity!» — a humorous epigram on Bloomsbury in the week-end competition of *The New Statesman and Nation*, December 10, 1949,[39] probably expresses most people's attitude adequately. Osbert Sitwell, who knew them all very well, points out in his *Laughter in the Next Room* that it was towards the disintegration of the Bloomsbury »Junta», as he facetiously calls them, that Bloomsbury, »under the genial vice-royalty of my friend Clive Bell, took a trend, hitherto unexpected, towards pleasure and fashionable life: but in these days (1918) it was still austere, with a degree of quaker earnestness latent in it».[40] Indeed, it is only fair to the majority of the set to stress their earnestness. For all their wittiness and outward frivolity, they held sacred the things that mattered to them: loyalty to their own principles in life, sincerity in art and in personal relationships.

All of them, however, were conscious of forming an élite, of belonging to those »who have a sensitiveness to purely formal relations (in art). To such people these relations have meaning and arouse keen emotions of pleasure».[41] It lifts them above the majority from whose standards they are conscious of differing

---

[37] 21. 6. 28, No. 1377, p. 465; cf. also *The Dial*, June 1929, Vol. LXXXVI. No. 6. pp. 518—20. A Fanfare from Bloombury by Alyse Gregory; The *Criterion* Sept. 1928, Vol. VIII. No. 30, pp. 161 ff. T. S. Eliot on Clive Bell's *Civilization*.

[38] idem

[39] E. W. Fordham, Vol. 38, No. 979, p. 710

[40] *Laughter in the Next Room*, p. 19

[41] Roger Fry: *The Artist and Psycho-Analysis*, p. 9

fundamentally also in the respect that they prefer an appeal to the intellect rather than solely to the senses. As intellectuals, they feel their responsibility very deeply as the trustees of civilization. Leonard Woolf, a serious and sincere person, — to take one example of the many — agrees with Clive Bell on the primary concern of a civilized nucleus being not with getting things done, with politics and power, but with things of the mind, in which he includes not only truth, speculation, and art, but also morality which was discarded by Bell. Pursuit of truth, Woolf says, is the most important of them, »regardless of consequence and in the teeth of one's own passions and prejudices»,[42] with Plato, Socrates, and Aristotle as models. With justification he points out how it happens time and again that »the highbrows of a certain generation hail a new writer, painter, or composer as an artist of eminence, while the great heart of the public of that generation refuses to be entertained, educated, pleased, or uplifted by him. Controversy rages and dies down; a new generation of highbrows and Frankaus[43] and great public is entertained, educated, pleased, and uplifted by those very works of art which the highbrows of the previous generation were derided and hunted for praising.»[44] And, indeed, Leonard and Virginia Woolf, for instance, may be justly proud of having among their protégées such artists as Katherine Mansfield, whose short stories they were the first to value and to publish, T. S. Eliot, Stephen Spender, Elizabeth Bowen, Rosamond and John Lehmann who have since all won their places in the sun, but who were unknown beginners when the Woolfs took them up. They saw, too, though not uncritically, the importance of Freud and his doctrines. The Hogarth Press was the first to publish whole series of psychoanalytical treatises. A most illuminating proof of the truth of Mr. Woolf's word is, however, the case of the Post-Impressionists whose works were exhibited

---

[42] L. Woolf: *Quack, Quack*, p. 110
[43] Mr. Gilbert Fraukau had written an attack on the highbrows in *An Author's Feelings on Publication Day*, hence his name in Mr. Woolf's article.
[44] L. Woolf: *Hunting the Highbrow*, p. 14

in London in 1910 for the first time through the efforts of Roger Fry, their ardent advocate. It almost gives one a shock to read the criticisms in the papers of those days; the derision is unbelievable. Now, forty years later, most people who are supposed to understand anything about art go and gaze at the Picassos and van Goghs reverently, even the very same people who derided them in 1910.

By 1928, when both Clive Bell's *Civilization* and Virginia Woolf's *Orlando* were first published, the Bloomsbury coterie had grown to be »a kind of group dictatorship of brains»,[45] as Frank Swinnerton — rather acidly, but with some justification undoubtedly — puts it, with Virginia Woolf as the central figure. In the preface to her *Orlando* she thanks her friends for their help. Although the preface may be considered a kind of family joke in its mock solemnity, we may assume that the list contains roughly the names of the people who were most often seen at the Bloomsbury homes.[46] They have their own jargon and their own idiosyncrasies of behaviour and humour which are naturally apt to irritate the outsiders. Osbert Sitwell gives an amusing, but affectionate description of them in his *Laughter in the Next Room*.[47] Frank Swinnerton, again, is scathing in his judgment. »Ostentatious refinement», he says, »is a part of its assertion of superiority; and I have so long believed all ostentation to be vulgar that I am sure Bloomsbury, at heart, is vulgar. It loves the eighteenth century — the wits, you know — and is fashionably coarse in its conversation. — It dresses distinctively and — in the female part of it — does its hair as Mrs. Gaskell used to do hers a hundred years ago, wearing long earrings and in some way managing always to look sickly. When it laughs, it grimaces desperately; for its laughter is painfully self-conscious. It speaks with great affectation, introducing all the vowels into so simple a word as 'no'. It is conversationally insincere, what one would call 'strained'; but although its tones are the tones of wit I constantly

---

[45] op. cit., p. 253
[46] Cf. Preface to *Orlando*
[47] op. cit., pp. 18—22

hear far wittier talk at my club, where men think less of showing off than of contributing to general gaiety. It is very sensitive and sarcastic ('ahrony'); is full of jealous contempts; is spiteful and resents being ignored, although it goes in a good deal for the wilful ignoring of others. And it has the impudence to accuse all who do not support its pretensions to superiority of being either fatuous or of selling the pass to the enemy. The enemy is Democracy.»[48] It is a good caricature of Bloomsbury, drawn with plenty of malice and some truth. But its irony was probably wasted on Bloomsbury, for they were quite capable of seeing themselves in a humorous light. As early as 1915, when Virginia Woolf had published her first novel, *The Voyage Out*, she had looked at herself and her friends with a smile: »It's what I've always said about literary people» — (this is Clarissa Dalloway writing to her friend) — »they're far the hardest of any to get on with. The worst of it is, these people — a man and his wife and a niece — might have been, one feels, just like everybody else, if they hadn't got swallowed up by Oxford or Cambridge or some such place, and been made cranks of. The man's really delightful (if he'd cut his nails), and the woman has quite a fine face, only she dresses, of course, in a potato sack, and wears her hair like a Liberty shopgirl's. They talk about art, and think us such poops for dressing in the evening. However, I can't help that, I'd rather die than come in to dinner without changing — wouldn't you? It matters ever so much more than the soup.»[49]

Virginia Woolf had gradually developed from the faithful listener that she was at the beginning of this century into the most important figure of the whole circle. It was round her that the activities centred. Her austere beauty, her distinguished personality with its bubbling humour and at the same time severely questioning spirit which was never satisfied with anything second-hand, ungenuine, which was always after the ultimate truths and the deepest stirrings of the human mind, gave the friendly gatherings their fascination and their

---

[48] op. cit., pp. 253—254
[49] *The Voyage Out*, p. 51

ton. When she died in 1941, something vanished that could not be replaced. The group, such as it was, came to an end. But its influence is still being felt. Books like *Olivia* will be published in which »the amateurs of exquisite states of mind» may find an atmosphere congenial to their spirits. Those books will perhaps even in the far future be said to remind the reader of something essentially Bloomsbury.

IV

Bloomsbury To-day

So, the world of Bloomsbury has come to an end. At the moment it is neither topical nor yet historical: an awkward moment for its critics to write about it. Personal likes and dislikes still weigh in valuations more heavily than objective criticism should allow, and the present phase in the changing world is not particularly suited for measuring the achievement of an intellectual aristocracy bearing a stamp of aestheticism. The younger generation, reared in a period of wars, are inclined to bestow on the citizens of that dying world the description Angus Wilson made popular with his collection of short stories: aesthetes — Bloomsbury or other — are Such Darling Dodos, an extinct race. The general feeling seems to be that the world of to-day cannot afford feeding that species any longer; they belong to the age of stability and prosperity as part of its luxuries. A critical attitude is thus gaining ground, but has not yet entirely ousted more sympathetic feelings: admiration and nostalgia are not by any means dead.

In 1948, in its leader of July 17th, *The Times Literary Supplement* took up to discuss Bloomsbury. Its article was called *Bloomsbury and Beyond* and was meant to be a kind of stock-taking of the set's importance. It is not only interesting as such, but also as an expression of the average opinion in the country. *The Times Literary Supplement* is a respected paper and its anonymous reviewers are believed to be experts in their respective fields; its opinion therefore carries weight.

It is characteristic of the fashionable attitude towards Bloomsbury to-day that even *The T. L. S.* gives a slightly distorted view of the content of its message. The writer calls Bloomsbury »the home of a set, a sounding-board of literary propaganda»,[1] but quite rightly points out that strictly speaking it was not what one might call a group, as it had no definite standpoint or common ground. Yet he generalizes without distinguishing clearly its main exponents — Virginia Woolf, E. M. Forster,[2] and Lytton Strachey, for instance — from those lesser lights thanks to whom the name has come to stand in the common opinion mainly for preciousness, pretentiousness, and snobbery. In the same way as the imitators have been a handicap to the right appreciation of T. S. Eliot's poetry, so has the unessential in Bloomsbury been confused with its real message. For instance, when the writer of the leader stamps the Bloomsbury set as kill-joys of art, the reader is slightly bewildered. »Round the century», he says, »'Bloomsbury' was not yet calling attention to its melancholy self by passionate rejection of anything approaching enjoyment in art».[3] It seems to be a misrepresentation of anything the main exponents ever wrote. From what follows, we gather that he must have had T. S. Eliot and his followers mainly in his mind, but Eliot was never very closely attached to the set and by no means an interpreter of its spirit. On the contrary, he is far too dogmatic in his beliefs to have been truly Bloomsbury at any point of his career, although, as a critic put it, »his figures have the quality of a saint in them and yet are acceptable at Bloomsbury cocoa parties».[4] We cannot, thus. entirely accept the writer's 'it' to mean Bloomsbury when he goes on with his interpretation. »Its roots», he says, »were in the disorder of society: the traditions of social life, of religion,

---

[1] July 17. 1948, No. 2424, p. 401

[2] Stephen Spender, in his *World Within World*, does not include E. M. Forster in Bloomsbury. In my article in the Finnish magazine *Valvoja*, No. 6 1951, pp. 257 ff., I have tried to prove that E. M. Forster, though subtle and original, bears the unmistakable Bloomsbury stamp in what he has to say. Also Noel Annan places Forster at least on the fringe of the set; cf. Annan, *Leslie Stephen*, p. 123, note.

[3] July 17, 1948, No. 2424, p. 401

[4] Harold Hobson in *The Observer*, Jan. 1, 1950

morals, literature had broken from their moorings. All things were adrift, said 'Bloomsbury', all things but itself. 'Bloomsbury' was anchored firmly in the faith that nothingness was the destiny of lost mankind. Because some real artists had made their intimations difficult, 'Bloomsbury' made a fetish of obscurity, in tune with the conviction that experience was without meaning.»[5] And so on, in the same misleading wein. It is not surprising that the article caused a mildly ironic protest by Lytton Strachey's brother, Oliver Strachey, who mentioned the names of his brother, J. M. Keynes, Roger Fry, Clive and Vanessa Bell, Leonard and Virginia Woolf, David Garnett, Desmond MacCarthy, E. M. Forster, Francis Birrell, and Arthur Waley as members of the group he had learned to know as Bloomsbury, and pointed out with justification how absurd it was to accuse them as the writer of the leader had done. The editor politely retreated and admitted in his answer the mistake of not making a distinction »between those distinguished writers and painters who lived — in some cases still live — in Bloomsbury, and the rank and file of nonentities who, for nearly twenty years, attracted to themselves what reflected glory they might from the luminaries of W. C. 1.».[6]

Part of the older generation had never liked Bloomsbury; a coterie like this is always bound to rouse antagonism, whether justified or not, and Bloomsbury, on their part, never did anything to fight the accusation of snobbery and superiority; on the contrary, fond of caricaturing as they were themselves, they rather enjoyed the exaggerated pictures drawn of them and even encouraged the attackers.[7] Yet, on the deaths of eminent Bloomsbury represen-

---

[5] T. L. S. July 17, 1948, No. 2424, p. 401

[6] ibid., July 31, 1948, No. 2426, p. 429

[7] Bloomsbury lacked solemnity and pathos and liked exaggeration and slight distortion. Examples of this Lytton Stracheyish trait may easily be found in all of them: Mr. Ramsay is a slightly distorted Leslie Stephen, in *To the Lighthouse*, Maynard Keynes has been accused of exaggeration in his *Essays in Persuasion*, or *Economic Consequences* (Cf., e.g., F. R. Leavis' article *Keynes, Lawrence and Cambridge* in *Scrutiny* Vol. XVI. No. 3 p. 246,

tatives, of persons like Virginia Woolf or Lord Keynes, long praising articles on Bloomsbury influence have appeared on the pages of respected daily papers and literary magazines. Even if part of the praise must be ascribed to the In-Memoriam-mood of the occasion, Bloomsbury is being found to have been an important corner of civilization. Not only are those who used to frequent the Bloomsbury homes becoming more and more nostalgic,[8] but also people who never belonged to the Sitwellian world of eccentrics and wits are seeing with regret the passing of the old world with its aristocratic ideals of spirit.

What has been happening in the last decade has contributed to counteract the Bloomsbury ideal of an intellectual élite with its 'vision' as a means to personal salvation. The war years have first of all enlarged the content of humanity, in width, at any rate; whether in depth, is a different matter. To most people it does not seem right to exclude so much of life as Virginia Woolf, for instance, does in her novels, or to hedge of people as rigidly as E. M. Forster. It does not do any more to elevate art at the expense of life as the aesthetes of Bloomsbury brand were inclined to do. There are some people who even begin asking — a gross sacrilege in some other people's ears — whether the rather melodramatic presentation of human experience in E. M. Forster's world is broad enough to entitle us to call his art great. Is it not pleasant carpentering rather than chiselling in nobler materials? And yet E. M. Forster stands, in the general estimation, on a much higher pedestal than Virginia Woolf. And where is Lytton Strachey at this moment? Practically nowhere at all. The targets

---

reprinted in *The Common Pursuit* pp. 255 ff.); Bell's *Civilization* abounds in it, even Bertrand Russell is not free from the foible either.

[8] Stephen Spender in his *World Within World* calls Bloomsbury »the most constructive and creative influence on English taste between the two wars«. (p. 140). He gives a fair and illuminating account on the set on pages 139 ff. So does also Noel Annan in *Leslie Stephen*, pp. 123 ff. and R. F. Harrod in his work on Lord Keynes, pp. 172 ff. Elizabeth Bowen, in her *Collected Impressions*, p. 79, also speaks with admiration about the vanished world of Bloomsbury. Cf. also Rose Macaulay in *The Spectator*, April 11, 1941, Vol. 5885, p. 394.

of his irony, the Victorians, are, instead, beginning to hold their own. The values are changing, the focus is being removed from the individual to the masses. Nothing is more natural. In war even death and suffering, those primarily and pre-eminently individual happenings, become mass events. »Mr. Ramsay stumbling along a passage stretched his arms out one dark morning, but Mrs. Ramsay having died rather suddenly the night before, he stretched his arms out. They remained empty.»[9] Such modest tones in expressing a great sorrow must sound lukewarm in comparison with the descriptions of all the sufferings that have to be borne in the wars. Yet there is no scale for measuring sorrow. A dull aching of a lonely heart has but few alleviating ingredients; mass sorrows, maybe, have their mass moments of elevation.

Whatever else the wars may have done, they have certainly shaken intelligent people's consciences and increased their sense of moral responsibility. Instead of an aesthetic attitude to life and consequently to literature, a moral and social attitude is now by a great many considered the proper one.[10] Hence the ousting of the world of Bloomsbury — at least temporarily. It is as remote, in F. L. Lucas's words,[11] as »shepherds' piping in Arcadia». The comparison is a specially happy one: it conveys the clarity of the Bloomsbury voice as well as its thinness. If that voice sounds like shepherds' sweet but thin piping to those who were lucky enough to hear it at close quarters, how much more so for people who only hear the

---

[9] *To the Lighthouse*, pp. 199—200

[10] Cf., e.g. Edwin Muir, *The Decline of the Imagination*, *The Listener*, May 10, 1951, Vol. XLV, No. 1158, pp. 753 ff.; F. L. Lucas, *Literature and Psychology*, Cassell & Co., 1951; Lionel Trilling, *The Liberal Imagination*, Secker & Warburg, 1951; Martin Turnell, *The Novel in France*, 1950. Or such haphazardly chosen examples as statements by Storm Jameson in *The Writer/s Situation*, 1950, p. 36; L. H. Myers, Preface to *The Root and the Flower*, pp. 9—10; Thomas Mann defends the Artist's aesthetic attitude as a primary duty, in *The Listener*, June 5, 1952, pp. 911 ff. He would thus side with Bloomsbury.

[11] in a private letter to the writer of this.

vanishing echo of the bodiless music! No wonder they are left straining their ears, especially as the bustle and upheavals of the modern world with its extra burden of mass sufferings are quenching the thin voice of »sweet reasonableness» which echoes the bliss of »exquisite states of mind». The distance from Virginia Woolf's death in 1941 seems, in fact, much longer than it is in years.

V

Father and Daughter as Critics

Moral sensibility is thus, it seems, ousting aesthetic sensibility in the present-day estimation of values and, consequently, as a qualification in a reviewer of literature. It is not, therefore, surprising to see a critic like Sir Leslie Stephen being heaved up from temporary oblivion.[1] He stands in the line with Dr. Johnson, Coleridge and

---

[1] In this connection it may be of interest to refer to certain attacks on Bloomsbury, as Leslie Stephen has been mentioned as a point of comparison. Bloomsbury's ethical and aesthic attitudes — their inheritance of Cambridge (vide Lord Keynes' *Two Memoirs*), — is unfavourably compared with what is by the attackers — F. R. Leavis, of Downing College, Cambridge, and his wife, Q. D. Leavis — called the real Cambridge spirit: the inheritance of Leslie Stephen's ethical attitudes, not of the aestheticism of the Lytton Stracheys or Desmond MacCarthys against whose Clarke Lecture on Leslie Stephen Q. D. Leavis's article, *Leslie Stephen, Cambridge Critic*, Scrutiny, March 1939, pp. 404 ff., is especially aimed. Q. D. Leavis had earlier shown her somewhat peevish and self-righteous sarcasm in dealing with Virginia Woolf's *Three Guineas*, Scrutiny, Sept. 1938, pp. 203 ff. Her husband has his say when reviewing Lord Keynes' *Two Memoirs*. He compares the two Cambridges, that of Leslie Stephen and of Lytton Strachey to the disadvantage of the latter and to the depreciation of Lord Keynes who had celebrated it in his *Memoirs*. »Can we imagine», Leavis asks, »Sidgwick or Leslie Stephen or Maitland being influenced by, or interested in, the equivalent of Lytton Strachey? By what steps and by the operation of what causes, did so great a change come over Cambridge in so comparatively short a time?» (Scrutiny, Sept. 1949 p. 246). It is interesting to note that the heaviest blows against Bloomsbury are coming from Cambridge where the Utilitarians of the Leavis-brand exist side by side with the former more or less faithful Bloomsbury-haunters: Sir John Sheppard is Provost of King's, E. M. Forster, F. L. Lucas, G. Rylands, and Noel Annan Fellows of King's. Cf. Annan, on the subject in *Leslie Stephen*, chapter IX, pp. 249 ff.

Matthew Arnold who considered literature to be »a criticism of life».[2] Leslie Stephen subscribed to this with great emphasis as an »undeniable truth».[3] For him, poetry and philosophy were twins, almost identical twins. »Under every poetry there lies philosophy», he writes in *Hours in a Library*.[4] »The poet and philosopher are interested in the same truths. What is the nature of man and the world in which he lives, and what, in consequence, should be our conduct? The difference is that the poet has intuitions while the philosopher gives demonstrations, that the thought which in one mind is converted into emotion, is in the other resolved into logic and that a symbolic representation of the idea is substituted for a direct expression. — In each case the highest intellectual faculty manifests itself in the vigour with which certain profound conceptions of the world and life have been grasped and assimilated.» The 'aesthetic' attitude of Pater, Symonds and the rest of them, was alien to the trend of his mind which distrusted theorizing, put its faith in the use of reason and propagated the scientific, inductive method in criticism.» That man», he says, »is the greater poet whose imagination is most transfused with reason, who has the deepest truths to proclaim as well as the strongest feelings to utter. Some theorists implicitly deny this principle by holding substantially that the poet's function is simply the utterance of a particular mood, and, that, if he utters it forcibly and delicately, we have no more to ask. Even so, we should not admit that the thoughts suggested to a wise man by a prospect of death and eternity are of just equal value, if equally well expressed, with the thoughts suggested to a fool by the contemplation of a good dinner. But, in practice, the utterance of emotions can hardly be dissociated from the assertion of principles.»[5] A great many present-day critics and writers would probably sign that statement.[6]

---

[2] *Essays in Criticism*, p. 249
[3] *Studies of a Biographer*, I. 91
[4] on Wordsworth's Ethics, III, pp. 178—9
[5] ibid., pp. 180—1
[6] cf. previous chapter, p. 66, note 10.

But Leslie Stephen was a temperate critic: he would probably have refused to go to such lengths in appreciating the mere utilitarian values of a work of art as I. A. Richards and his school.[7] He never discarded the pleasure-value to the extent Tolstoy, for instance did in his *What is Art*. In spite of the fact that Stephen had in his youth been greatly influenced by J. S. Mill's utilitarian ideas, any rigid application of them in art was as uncongenial to him as was Pater's aestheticism. He was shy of any administering of a fixed code of law supposed to be applicable in all times and places, though he did not deny that there are some principles of universal application. He always insisted on facts to prove the specific case. In the work of the critic, giving information was to him more important than mere praise, even when well-earned. »The critic», he says, »before abandoning himself to the oratorical impulse, should endeavour to classify the phenomena with which he is dealing as calmly as if he were ticketing a fossil in a museum. The most glowing eulogy, the most bitter denunciation, have their proper place; but they belong to the art of persuasion, and form no part in scientific method. Our faith in an author must, in the first instance, be the product of instinctive sympathy, instead of deliberate reason. But when we are seeking to justify our emotions, we must endeavour to get for the time into the position of an independent spectator, applying with rigid impartiality such methods as are best calculated to free

---

[7] I. A. Richards was also a Cambridge man at the time he published his important *Principles of Literary Criticism* (1925). It was there that Richards tried to explode the idea of an aesthetic approach to art and declared the concepts of 'beauty' and 'pure aesthetic value' to be myths. A work of art, according to him, must be judged on the basis of the value of mental experience it offers us, and, secondly, of the efficacy with which that experience is communicated. Richards's theories enjoyed wide popularity in the 'thirties'. Those who accepted them, naturally turned against Bloomsbury aestheticism as propagated by Roger Fry and Clive Bell. A great many remained followers of the new utilitarian literary mode for a time; it was like an attack of measles — inevitable in young critics, but the sooner got over the better. Most critics returned to the safe middle path accepting both the 'influence-value' and the 'pleasure-value' in a work of art.

us from the influence of personal bias. Undoubtedly it is a very difficult task to be alternately witness and judge; to feel strongly, and yet to analyse coolly, to love every feature in a familiar face, and yet to decide calmly upon its ugliness or beauty...».[8] It cannot be said that Leslie Stephen himself always managed to preserve the unbiased attitude. He had strong likes and dislikes, but he tried hard to be fair, yet remain outspoken. »The more hard-hitting goes on in the world the better I am pleased — meaning always hard-hitting in the spiritual sense»,[9] he wrote (of Huxley). For all his love of Dr. Johnson, he called *The Rambler* »unreadable, unendurable stuff»,[10] and Johnson's style »a work of bad art».[11] On the other hand, for all his dislike of Sterne, he praised in generous words his stylistic strength: »One can hardly read the familiar passages without admitting that Sterne was perhaps the greatest artist in the language»,[12] an opinion that was later enthusiastically signed by Virginia Woolf in one of her best essays.[13] Leslie Stephen could be very sharp-tongued, but almost invariably he came forward with a sincere apology if, on second thoughts, he felt that he had been too harsh. So for instance in the case of F. D. Maurice whom he had called »a muddle-headed, intricate, futile person».[14] It is Maurice that he has in mind when he writes, in *Social Rights and Duties*: »I have often enough spoken too harshly and vehemently of my antagonists. I have tried to fix upon them too unreservedly what seemed to me the logical consequences of their dogmas. I have condemned their attempts at a milder interpretation of their own creed as proofs of insincerity, when I ought to have done more justice to the legitimate and lofty motives which prompted them.»[15] It is a very human and sympathetic Leslie

---

[8] on Ch. Brontë in *Hours in a Library*, III. 326
[9] *Studies of a Biographer*, III. 202
[10] *Hours in a Library*, II. 212
[11] ibid., p. 216
[12] ibid., IV. 57
[13] Introduction to *A Sentimental Journey*, included in *The Common Reader* II, pp. 78 ff.
[14] Letter to Norton 30. 3. 74 quoted in Maitland, p. 240
[15] ibid., p. 260

Stephen that steps towards us from the pages of his letters and essays. It is interesting to see Leslie Stephen's results from his application of the inductive method. He, like Virginia Woolf,[16] has an eye for large vistas: he places the man in his background, and often begins his critical approach from the outer circumstances. Johnsonese, thus, is in his opinion as much a part of Johnson's entity as his legs, an opinion which differs from that of Macaulay who considered Johnsonese as part of a definite literary theory. Stephen's connecting Johnson's queer jargon with a larger view is however entirely in keeping with modern trends of criticism. He sees in it »the natural expression of certain innate tendencies, and of mental atmosphere which he breathed from youth».[17] He also places Johnson's literary failure against a larger horizon: born into the right century, he might have been as great a writer as he was a talker. As it was, »the fashionable costume of the day hampered the free exercise of his powers», and the only creeds to which he could attach himself were passing through a phase of decline and inanition. »A century earlier or later he might have succeeded in expressing himself through books as well as his talk; but it is not given to us to choose the time of our birth and some very awkward consequences follow.»[18] Autobio-

---

[16] In Virginia Woolf's essays we find her constantly describing »what sort of person the writer is», stressing his perspective as an integral factor in a work of art and letting his physical presence steal through. She thus joins those critics who consider that a work of art should not be detached from its background. For her, the aesthetic theory of pure art is not enough in criticism. Beside the technical aspects pertaining to a work of art she recognizes those elements which must be approached from a psychological angle to be rightly understood: imagery, for instance, or social vision, or the question of values. She represented in fact what Herbert Read calls 'genetic criticism' (in *Annals of Innocence and Experience*, p. 117). Fundamentally Virginia Woolf did not believe in 'art for art's sake'. In theory, at any rate, she considered it her job not only to illuminate experience and to convey it to her reader, but also »to choose her patron wisely» (vide *The Patron and the Crocus*, *The Common Reader* I, pp. 261 ff.) so as to reach him with her message.

[17] *Hours in a Library* II, p. 202

[18] ibid., p. 421

graphical elements in books, the mental make-up of the author, come under Stephen's scrutiny whenever possible. He even goes to the lengths that remind us of Virginia Woolf's over-emphatic statement in *Orlando* when she says: »Every secret of a writer's soul, every experience of his life, every quality of his mind is written large in his works.»[19] When speaking about the Brontës, Leslie Stephen exclaims: »Nobody ever put so much of themselves into their work.»[20] However objective a writer professes to be, he always betrays his own secrets, »is his own Boswell», in Leslie Stephen's words; he finds that the autobiographical element in many of the best novels contributes to deepening the feeling and to raising the book above the purely imaginary novel. That happens, for instance, in *Robinson Crusoe*. Stephen credits Defoe with a powerful but limited imagination. His strength lies in his amazing talent for telling lies. If he is artistic, as in *Robinson Crusoe*, he is that, as it were, in spite of himself, because of the very autobiographical affinity of the story: the island is Defoe's own solitude in prison. On the other hand, Stephen warns against the great dangers of using autobiographical stuff because of its easiness in giving vent to one's feelings: Hazlitt's *Liber Amoris* or Charlotte Brontë's books serve as examples. The latter's work suffered materially from the comparative narrowness of the circle of ideas in which her mind habitually revolved. »The comparative eclipse of Charlotte Brontë», Stephen says, »does not imply want of power, but want of comprehensiveness. — The power of grasping general truths is necessary to give a broad base to a writer's fame, though his capacity for tender and deep emotion is that which makes us love or hate him».[21]

What has been said above may suffice to give some kind of picture of Leslie Stephen's quality as a critic[22] and to serve as a starting-point of comparison in the attempt to elucidate his daughter's essayistic and critical work. Leslie Stephen is a solid and reliable

---

[19] *Orlando*, pp. 189—190
[20] *Hours in a Library* III, p. 333
[21] ibid., pp. 328—9
[22] For further elucidation see Noel Annan, op.cit.

critic, genuine and honest, an original but a somewhat heavy thinker. Virginia Woolf in the inheritrix of his talents, but adds to them her mother's — and her own — elf-like qualities. She has the magic wand of a born creator, which Leslie Stephen lacks. In her essays, too, she is first and foremost an imaginative writer in whose hands a dry piece of information begins shooting green leaves and flowers, and soon we see her, butterfly-like, fluttering among them, hardly seeming to touch their petals, yet helping to create new life.

To a great many readers Virginia Woolf means an artist who concentrates on *how* to say things to such an extent that *what* is said is dimmed to an undue degree. Only in her essays do they find a balance suited to their tastes, consequently these enjoy greater popularity than her novels. Perhaps it is true that in her novels Virginia Woolf demands a great deal more of concentrated attention than the common reader considers fair and is willing to give. The 'uncommon' reader, however, may find a constant source of delight in them. The critics, too, disagree a great deal. There are some who deny sufficient creative impulse in the novels and stamp them as the attempts of an essayist, not instinctively a novelist, to use fiction as a means of expression. Thus Henry Sampson, for instance; Virginia Woolf's essays, »traditional in form and theme», he says, »have far more genuine impulse than her novels, which carry little conviction as vital creations.»[23] He, thus, joins those who criticise Virginia Woolf for small invention and a lack in »the emotional depth of an imaginative person».[24] [25]

In so far as Virginia Woolf's characters are claimed to be embodiments of her ideas, it is easy to agree with the critics — though Sampson's epithets, »transient and embarrassed phantoms»,[26] are

---

[23] *The Concise Cambridge History of English Literature*, XV. 975; cf. also Martin Turnell on V. W. in *Horizon* Vol. VI. No. 31 July 1942, p. 44

[24] Frank Swinnerton, op. cit., p. 282

[25] Also cf. Edmund Wilson, in *Axel's Castle*, p. 123; he accuses Virginia Woolf's critical work of sterility and pedantry, lumping it together with Lytton Strachey's and Clive Bell's essays.

[26] loc. cit.

challengeable. The impression is unavoidable that she chooses the characters in her novels in the same way that she selects the subjects of her essays: to elaborate some theory, to create an effect. She is a conscious artist — but not necessarily a lesser artist for that, though there is a danger in her method of interpreting, as it were, her own creations. She can, with some justification, be accused of not letting her characters alone, freely to grow and develop according to their own laws of personality. In a way her Christina Rossettis, Pastons, Geraldines, Janes and the rest of them, are embellished with traits which need not necessarily be taken as gospel truths, so, too, the Ramsays and Septimus Smiths are projections of their creator's own personality. In that respect her invention may indeed be called small in width: she is writing down herself. But, she may retort quoting herself: »Beyond the difficulty of communicating oneself, there is the supreme difficulty of being oneself.»[27] Every line in Virginia Woolf's work is a reflection of an original mind; her insight, the felicitous touches in character building, the aptness of phrasing, the point of view are that of a born creator. Mrs. Ramsay, in spite of being an embodiment of Virginia Woolf's idea of a woman's 'good life', cannot be denied independent existence as a creation of art. Delattre, to take an example of appreciative criticism, sees in Virginia Woolf first and foremost an authentic creator. »Les essais critiques de Virginia Woolf», he says, »ne représentent qu'une sorte d'avant-propos de son oeuvre. — Ces qualités, une erudition délicate, une inspiration sincère, moins proprement critiques que créatrices déjà —».[28] Although Delattre's opinion is the reverse of Sampson's, both are pointing, in a way, to the same fact, namely, that the essays are closely linked to Virginia Woolf's other work: she is expressing in both her innermost self.

Virginia Woolf's critical work preceded her novelist's career and later overlapped it at every point. She was not one of those who, in Landor's words, after failing as writers turn reviewers. She

---

[27] *The Common Reader* I, p. 86
[28] *Le roman psychologique de Virginia Woolf*, p. 79

was thirty-three when, in 1915, she published her first novel, *The Voyage Out*, on which she had been working for seven years. While preparing her novel she practised her hand at sketches and reviews for various English and American periodicals. From the beginning we detect in them without difficulty Leslie Stephen's daughter, well read — she had not been let loose in her father's library from her earliest years for nothing — with an agile mind and an agile pen, used to travelling to and fro in the realms of widely different minds like a native of each realm, moving in and out without needing to bother about passports and visas, the encumbrances of ordinary travellers. The strange Elizabethans as well as the Victorians, Sterne's Ghost as well as a Mary Wollstonecraft or a Laetitia Pilkington, the French authors as well as the Russians, come into the sphere of her interest. The personality behind the book fascinates Virginia Woolf as much as what is in the book. The complexity of human beings, the wealth of human minds stimulate her. She uncovers the greatness of the small and the smallness of the great. She is unorthodox in the selection of her material. A moth is as grateful an object for her imagination as an unknown woman in the train or a well-known book. Life, we are made to feel, is an adventure; a human being is free to go, to see, and to experience. Books are the vessels that carry us to the far-off lands, to the odd beasts and tropical flowers.

If Leslie Stephen's style strikes the reader as being a suitable cover to its solid, informative, reasoned message, Virginia Woolf's is also well-suited for its special task: the reader is surreptitiously swept away by its felicitousness for conveying, not so much ponderous content, as the author's own original angle of vision. Her touch is often light but as often as not covers a point of importance; superficiality, for all her lightness, is an accusation that only a superficial reader can throw against Virginia Woolf. She is not shy of unusual metaphors and surprising parallels; her humour is also readily at hand. The reader is thus kept amused and interested, for whether one agrees with her or not, she always has something fresh to say. Clever, short-cut implications make the reader anxious to find out more about the person or the event described. Exaggeration plays its definite part, and obviously contradictory statements are not uncommon, but they are presented with such a delightfully sweeping gesture that the reader passes them with a good-humoured smile. Exaggeration, we remember, is not an unknown trait in Leslie Stephen's essays nor in his mental make-up either, though he was fond of mildly rebuking his wife for that weakness. He would no doubt have said that it was from her that Virginia inherited that trait as well as her feminine irrationality. Whatever the origin, the fact is that hyperbole is one of Virginia Woolf's temptations. She likes to choose a feature, to let it swell slightly out of proportion, and to build a personality round it, especially if she is dealing with some less known personality whom she makes light up some special aspect in the background. She loves to take a Jack Mytton or a Selina Trimmer or Shakespeare's imaginary sister round whom she can safely spin her yarn and let her easily incited imagination loose — a thing that her father would not have consented to do, or even approved of in a critic. What information and reasoning were for Leslie Stephen, imagination and intuition are for Virginia Woolf.

It is a significant characterization that Virginia Woolf gives of her Common Reader;[29] he is distinguished, she says quoting Dr. Johnson, among other things and above all by the fact that he is »guided by an instinct to create for himself, out of whatever odds and ends he can come by, some kind of whole — a portrait of a man, a sketch of an age, a theory of the art of writing. He never ceases, as he reads, to run up some rickety and ramshackle fabric which shall give him temporary satisfaction of looking sufficiently like the real object to allow of affection, laughter, and argument».[30] One is probably justified in doubting whether this is the common reader's attitude, but it certainly is Virginia Woolf's. Her essays can indeed roughly be divided into the three groups: portraits of men, sketches

---

[29] The name of the first two collections of essays, which were the only ones she published herself; the three later ones are posthumous.
[30] *The Common Reader* I, p. 11

of an age, elucidations of theories of the art of writing; »affection, laughter, and argument» are there, so is »some rickety and ramshackle fabric».

As numerous references to her essays will follow, we shall here only take one example, her essay on Montaigne.[31] In many ways it is a specially illuminating piece of writing, for nowhere do Leslie Stephen's words about every author being his own Boswell hold good in a greater degree: Virginia Woolf, the personality, the essayist, the novelist, are there shown to be an inseparable entity. The very choice of the subject is revealing: she could not have selected anyone nearer to her own metal. In several respects Montaigne can be considered to have been a special pilot light for her. Consequently the essay is packed with points which help us to understand and elucidate her own quality of writing. The congeniality of the subject has also inspired her to write one of her very best essays.

Montaigne's essays portray him as an aristocratic master of the art of living, aristocratic in the best sense of the word: it is only by the well-born soul — l'âme bien née — that truth can be known, he claims. Despite his love of retirement into solitude to contemplate, he is ready to grant that the common man is important, that there are perhaps more of the qualities that matter among the ignorant than among the learned, or, as Virginia Woolf paraphrases: »We may enjoy our room in the tower, with the painted walls and the commodious bookcases, but down in the garden there is a man digging who buried his father this morning, and it is he and his like who live the real life and speak the real language.»[32] It is a painful feeling for one who wants both to retire into a tower and to mix with his fellow-beings; we shall meet Virginia Woolf lamenting her 'exile' in *Jacob's Room*. Her, like Montaigne's, business of life and of art is to communicate the soul. But how difficult the task of telling the truth about oneself is! »'tis a rugged road», Montaigne is quoted as saying, »more so than it seems, to follow a pace so ram-

---

[31] ibid., pp. 84—97
[32] ibid., p. 89

bling and uncertain, as that of the soul; to penetrate the dark profundities of its intricate internal windings; to choose and lay hold of so many little nimble motions; 'tis a new and extraordinary undertaking, and that withdraws us from the common and most recommended employments of the world.»[33] No one could feel a greater sympathy for Montaigne's efforts to communicate the vagaries of the soul than Virginia Woolf who knows the difficulties of expression from her own experience. »We all indulge», she says, »in the strange, pleasant process called thinking, but when it comes to saying, even to some one opposite, what we think, then how little we are able to convey! The phantom is through the mind and out of the window before we can lay salt on its tail, or slowly sinking and returning to the profound darkness which it has lit up momentarily with a wandering light.»[34] But, before we can communicate ourselves, there must be a personality to communicate. One of Montaigne's chief attractions for Virginia Woolf is the fact that he was so enchantingly himself, a free, courageous, independent personality, in the line with her dearest figures, the Ambroses and Ramsays who also passionately keep to their right of having »a private life» of their own, who are possessors of souls that are complex, full of mysterious contradictions, souls that are »the greatest monster and miracle in the world».[35] Life itself is found by Montaigne as well as by his interpreter to be irrational, full of change and movement which are »the essence of our being; rigidity is death; conformity is death; let us say what comes into our heads, repeat ourselves, contradict ourselves, fling out the wildest nonsense, and follow the most fantastic fancies without caring what the world does or thinks or says. For nothing matters except life; and, of course, order.»[36] In life, though no fact is too little to let it slip through our fingers, a balance must reign, freedom and order must fit in with each other, beauty and goodness

---

[33] ibid., p. 85
[34] idem
[35] ibid., p. 96
[36] ibid., pp. 90—91

must find their proper proportions, nearly identical. Only then can the mastery of life be said to have been achieved. And yet — Leslie Stephen's daughter remains slightly worried. Is this overwhelming interest in the nature of soul enough? Is beauty enough? Is communication enough? Virginia Woolf is less sure than Montaigne. There is no answer for her; she remains a questioner.

VI

First Novels

Toleration in human relationships — except for Philistines and Middlebrows — was highly rated in Bloomsbury. In art the matter was different. Virginia Woolf may have been shy of saying what she expected of other people and of life, but she knew exactly what she demanded of art and how she wanted things expressed. The grudge she bears against the Edwardians — Wells, Bennett, and Galsworthy in the lead — and their 'materialism', i.e. their method of crowding their novels with the unnecessary bric-à-brac of a Victorian drawing-room, with detailed descriptions of the outer world, was an old grievance with her. From the outset of her career as a writer, realism had meant something quite different for her; character was to be built from inside outwards and not the other way round, which, in her opinion, was the misguided method of the Edwardians as much as it had been of the Victorians. It is no wonder that Dickens, for instance, irritated her.

As early as 1919, Virginia Woolf had written an essay on *Modern Fiction*[1] which still remains the most-quoted, and most important elucidation of her theories on art and life. In that fairly youthful essay she stands practically where she was to remain all her life: her ideas got their shape at an early stage. There is development and experimenting in her method, but very little change in her basic ideas. Fundamentally she was a poet and a thinker, and once she had formulated her philosophy — such as it was — and found her form, there was development in depth rather than in breadth.

---

[1] *The Common Reader* I, pp. 184 ff.

Her novels and the essays dealing with her craft are but elaborations of what she had compressed into that short essay. A short passage is enough to give the true Virginia Woolf ring. »Look within», she says, »and life, it seems, is very far from being 'like this'. Examine for a moment an ordinary mind on an ordinary day. The mind receives a myriad impressions — trivial, fantastic, evanescent, or engraved with the sharpness of steel. From all sides they come, an incessant shower of innumerable atoms; and as they fall, as they shape themselves into the life of Monday or Tuesday, the accent falls differently from of old; the moment of importance came not here but there . . .»[2] And so on. There we already have the gist of *A Room of One's Own*, of *Jacob's Room*, *Mrs. Dalloway*, and *To the Lighthouse*, in fact, of every one of her novels between 1922 and 1941. She speaks almost with the energy of a pioneer farmer who has a virgin soil to cultivate. In a way, of course, she is breaking new ground, for she is one of the 'moderns', an interpreter of the age of disintegration, of the atomic age: splitting is the password. The tendency is manifested by the deepening interest in the analysis of human nature, in the desire to bomb the depths of the subconscious, to revalue the forces that form human society, to rearrange human relations. With these changes, views on almost everything — religion, conduct, politics, literature — were bound to be revised. Virginia Woolf and her friends were mainly of the opinion that the change was all to the good.

Bloomsbury remained, even after their youthful Cambridge days, surprisingly sanguine about their belief in the possibility of human rationality. They were inclined to sneer at Victorian wishful thinking and — to the Bloomsbury mind — childish faiths, but at the same time they developed wishful thinking and faiths of their own. Mainly they believed in not believing, yet they could not help cherishing a faith in the ultimate, though perhaps distant, arrival of a Voltairean millennium of reason. While waiting for its coming, they considered that the world could best be prepared for it by attributing the causes of existing evils to the structure of

---

[2] ibid., p. 189

society — a process that still continues. But by their belief in the power of reason Bloomsbury was as much dated back to the age of security, which they inherited from the much-abused Victorians, as the latter were linked to their century by their belief in a benevolent God who had chosen the British to hoist their Union Jack in as many remote corners of the world as possible — remote, but, preferably, rich in natural resources. Bloomsbury did not believe in the God of their fathers, nor in Empire-building and prosperity, nor in action and effort. Yet they enjoyed having the results of that prosperity at their disposal: the opportunities of contemplation, of refining sensibilities and cultivating personal relationships were accepted without pangs of conscience and very much as a matter of course: were the recipients not the chosen people, the nucleus of intelligentsia for whom leisure was as necessary as air? But it seems as if the world progressed through stages of action and reaction. Bloomsbury rebelled against the Victorians; the younger generation again seems to be reacting against them. Virginia Woolf has some penetrating things to say in her essay, *The Leaning Tower*,[3] which deals with the changes in ideas during the two generations and in the social consciences of the best of modern youth.

The age of insecurity, sprung on an unsuspecting world with the First World War, seems as yet to have produced no masterpieces. *Ulysses* has perhaps the nearest claim as the most typical product of the age, but its message is intelligible to so limited an audience that it cannot be classed together with, say, *War and Peace* or *Madame Bovary*. Yet interesting books have been written; there has been no lack of original talent. In Britain we need only mention some names: besides Joyce, there are T. S. Eliot, Aldous Huxley, D. H. Lawrence, there is Bloomsbury — Virginia Woolf, E. M. Forster, Lytton Strachey. But each writer seems to have a special bone to pick. »Masterpieces», Virginia Woolf pertinently points out, »are not single or solitary births: they are the outcome of many years of thinking in common, of thinking by the body of the people, so

---

[3] *The Moment and Other Essays*, pp. 106 ff.

that the experience of the mass is behind the single voice».[4] Though we could point out that real geniuses and prophets — an Ibsen, or a Nietzsche — are usually solitary rebels, what Virginia Woolf says in another essay, generalising slightly less exaggeratedly, seems to be proved by the general achievement, or rather non-achievement, of her own period. »Common beliefs», she says in *How It Strikes a Contemporary*, »in the earlier ages made it easier to write. To believe that your impressions hold good for others is to be released from the cramp and confinement of personality, — — the contemporary writers cannot generalize. They depend on their senses and emotions, whose testimony is trustworthy, rather than on their intellects whose message is obscure.»[5] It is a likely explanation for the fact that our authors remained single voices; there was, indeed, no thinking in common, no accepted meaning to communicate. As if in defiance, the authors developed a tendency to stress their individuality in all possible forms, some through the difficulty and obscurity of their message, others by choosing experimental methods of communication. Huxley turned satirical and bitter, Lawrence sank into his mysticism of sex, Forster gradually stopped writing fiction, Joyce and Virginia Woolf experimented with the inner monologue, the former descending to his private realm of the subconscious, the latter retiring into her private realm of refined sensibilities. It is interesting to note, as Daiches points out,[6] that the gradual movement away from the transitional period is characterized by a slowing down of experiments in technique and by a turning towards social issues, a trend clearly to be seen in the present-day novel.

»Modernism», a critic says of Virginia Woolf, »is in her bones».[7] She had indeed been endowed with a sensitive apparatus to catch what was in the air. Both the influences from outside and what was latent in her made her an experimenter. But when the same critic

---

[4] *A Room of One's Own*, p. 98
[5] *The Common Reader* I, p. 302
[6] *The Novel and the Modern World*, p. 16
[7] J. W. Beach, *The Twentieth Century Novel*, p. 490

goes on to saying that Virginia Woolf »can write novels, in many ways, in any way but the traditional one»,[8] he seems to have forgotten her first two attempts which are, surely, conventional enough in form. Desmond MacCarthy, for one, praised them as good novels, a praise he does not by any means lavish on her later, more experimental works. He is all for solid story-telling and regrets the prevailing tendency towards the abnormal and queer, towards »an artificial heightening of moments in the lives which they (modern serious novelists) describe, either because those moments illustrate some theory, or because they are queer. Nothing evaporates so quickly as the fascination of the queer, or dies sooner than a theory».[9] He has, consequently, very little patience with Joyce, and a much more limited amount of sympathy with Virginia Woolf's later achievement than, for instance Swinnerton would have us believe.[10] But *The Voyage Out* and *Night and Day* MacCarthy finds truly charming. And so, for many, they are. Charming and cultured, especially *The Voyage Out* of which a new Uniform Edition has recently (1950) been issued. Maybe some readers who have been scared of reading Virginia Woolf by her later, more difficult novels, will be pleasantly surprised if they venture to take up the book and to read it. It tells a straightforward story in the best Edwardian manner; there is hardly anything that might be called rebellious, though seeds of ideas may be detected which were later to yield a good crop.

A young, inexperienced girl, Rachel Vinrace, embarks upon a voyage out from her sheltered home in Richmond, makes a trip on her father's steamer to South America, falls in love with an eligible young man, becomes engaged to him, but dies of tropical fever before the trip is over. This, in one sentence, is the story of *The Voyage Out*, simple enough. But within that framework there is plenty of fine writing, good dialogue, interesting characters well drawn, not very much movement outwards, but plenty inwards

---

[8] idem
[9] *Criticism*, p. 156
[10] vide op. cit., p. 252

into the characters. States of mind are discussed at great length in a truly Bloomsbury manner. The scene is fairly static, as always in Virginia Woolf; in this book it is a ship and an hotel. The atmosphere is fresh, youthful, somehow moving. Rachel is very immature, but mainly under the influence of her wordly-wise aunt, Mrs. Ambrose (an early variety of Mrs. Ramsay — in this first novel we meet a great many characters that will appear in the later novels, though greatly changed) has every opportunity for developing into a harmonious personality. But death intervenes, as it almost invariably does in Virginia Woolf's novels. Rachel's death is not, as a critic[11] regretfully — and mistakenly — ascribes it to, a result of a weak concession on the author's part to the prevailing taste for tragedy as the end of a book. It is something much more fundamental in Virginia Woolf, as can be seen from a short passage describing Terence Hewet's watch at his fiancée's death-bed; it contains a great deal of what is essential in Virginia Woolf's later novels: »The longer he sat there the more profoundly was he conscious of the peace invading every corner of his soul. Once he held his breath and listened acutely; she was still breathing; he went on thinking for some time; they seemed to be thinking together; he seemed to be Rachel as well as himself; and then he listened again; no, she had ceased to breathe. It was happiness, it was perfect happiness. They had now what they had always wanted to have, the union which had been impossible while they lived. Unconscious whether he thought the words or spoke them aloud, he said, 'No two people have ever been so happy as we have been. No one has ever loved as we have loved'. It seemed to him that their complete union and happiness filled the room with rings eddying more and more widely. He had no wish in the world left unfulfilled. They possessed what could never be taken from them.»[12] The idea of complete happiness in life being impossible, of human relationships even at their best being imperfect, of death as the great unifier, is recurrent in Virginia Woolf. Yet it is not so

---

[11] R. Brimley Johnson: *Some Contemporary Novelists* (Women), p. 157
[12] *The Voyage Out*, p. 431

much a note of pessimism and futility that rings in those contemplations as the message T. S. Eliot expresses in his *Four Quartets* when he says: »In my end is my beginning». It is the cosmic circle, unity behind seeming polarity, life versus death, that are to become the leading themes in Virginia Woolf's books. Reality as shown by phenomena does not satisfy her; she wants to penetrate beyond them. For her, too, *Alles Vergängliche ist nur ein Gleichnis*. Like D. H. Lawrence, she wants to catch the 'otherness', though for her it has an entirely different content and is reached through creative and mystical contemplation, not through sex.

In her first novel Virginia Woolf is still groping to find her way; she has not yet decided upon the path she is going to take towards interpreting life and human beings. But there are already some important beacons lit to guide her way. Terence Hewet, Rachel's fiancé, is the author's mouthpiece in the book. His desire is to write a novel »about the things people don't say».[13] This reminds the reader of Virginia Woolf's great interest in Sterne whom she calls »a forerunner of the moderns».[14] Silence was to be one of her own leading themes too. Terence expresses another significant point in his creator's vision when he is made to say: »Things I feel come to me like lights. — — I want to combine them — —. Have you ever seen fireworks that make figures? — — I want to make figures.»[15] To make a prism out of the erratic flashes of colour, to create unity out of the seeming disorder in life, 'to make figures', was to be Virginia Woolf's aim. That there was unity, she felt sure, and she accepted the Aristotelian idea of an artist's task being to find the universal behind the particular. It is for her the only way towards understanding. »To see things without attachment, from the outside, and to realize their beauty in itself — how strange! And then the sense that a burden has been removed; pretence and make-believe and unreality are gone, and lightness has come with a kind of transparency, making oneself

---

[13] ibid., p. 262
[14] *The Common Reader* II, p. 81
[15] *The Voyage Out*, p. 266

invisible and things seen through as one walks — how strange!» she writes in *The Waves*.[16] But before she reached that stage of revelation and assurance, there was a long way to go. She was, time and again, compelled, like Lily Briscoe with her vision of things, to assert herself almost with passion, and to cry out: »This is how I see it!» Both Lily Briscoe and her creator know that the singleness of vision is not to be reached without sacrifices and constant effort. How to combine actuality and its hidden meaning was to be Virginia Woolf's crucial problem, the solution of which was not easy for the sceptically minded rationalist that she was by heredity and training. »One must keep on looking», she writes in *To the Lighthouse*, »without for a second relaxing the intensity of emotion, the determination not to be put off, not to be bamboozled. One must hold the scene — so — in a vice and let nothing come in and spoil it. One wanted — — to be on the level with ordinary experience, to feel simply that's a chair, that's a table, and yet at the same time, It's a miracle, it's an ecstasy. The problem might be solved after all.»[17] But Virginia Woolf can hardly be said to have solved it. Even in her last novel she is left conjecturing, guessing, unable and perhaps unwilling to accept any positive creed in metaphysical speculations. She remains a poet with open doors rather than a philosopher with fully formulated theories.[18]

The Voyage Out was its author's first quest for reality. The next novel, *Night and Day*, took another turning. In fact, Virginia Woolf is always taking fresh turnings. Every one of her novels is an attempt at something new. At this point of her career it was as if she had become scared of the audacity of her ambitions, as if she had laughed

---

[16] p. 288

[17] *To the Lighthouse*, pp. 309 ff.

[18] It has been said, notably by John Hawley Roberts in his very interesting study on VW and Roger Fry, *PMLA*, Sept. 1946, Vol. LXI, No. 3, pp. 835—47, that the problem was for VW, as well as for Roger Fry, purely a problem of form and as such solvable. He sees in VW's works a conscious realization of Roger Fry's theories. Cf. also Th. Jewell Craven in *The Dial*, July 1921, Vol. LXXI, No. 1, p. 101. The unity she is after seems to me, however, to consist of larger perspectives than the perfect order in the formal values of a beautiful picture would allow us to presume.

at herself a little and tried to curb her enthusiasm. *Night and Day* is largely in the vein of a comedy of manners. Both Jane Austen and E. M. Forster are obvious objects of comparison. It is the teapot that rules and the drawing-room that lends the atmosphere to the novel. But there is not that contrast between stupidity and intelligence which we meet in both Jane Austen and Forster. Mrs. Hilbery, though a comic character, is not Mrs. Bennett. Virginia Woolf's drawing-room is peopled with fairly intelligent members of the privileged classes who discuss with ready and witty retorts a friend's loss of faith in his theory of truth and other similar topics. The atmosphere is the one in which Virginia Stephen had been reared. The Alardyces and the Hilberys are a gifted family. »They had been conspicuous judges and admirals, lawyers and servants of the State for some years before the richness ot the soil culminated in the rarest flower that any family can boast, a great writer, a poet among the poets of England, a Richard Alardyce; and having produced him, they proved once more the amazing virtues of their race by proceeding unconcernedly again with their usual task of breeding distinguished men».[19] It is clearly the world of, say, the Stephens and the Stracheys. Phrase-making runs in the family, though Katherine Hilbery, the heroine of the novel, is given to the secret vice of solving mathematical problems in the solitude of her room. She cannot decide whether to marry William Rodney who is »half a poet, half an old maid»,[20] or Ralph Denham, a solicitor and »not quite a gentleman»,[21] who has the endearing quality of knowing Sir Thomas Browne's works by heart. Consequently she becomes engaged to the former and ends by marrying the latter. There is plenty of comedy: the criss-crossing of the lovers' paths, Rodney reading his paper on Elizabethan metaphor in poetry to a youthful, but discriminating audience in Mary Datchet's ascetic room. For all her feminism, Virginia Woolf also pokes good-humoured fun at those who are »at it» from ten to six every day, i.e., at the organized vehemence of the suffragette

[19] *Night and Day*, p. 30
[20] ibid., p. 64
[21] idem

movement. She does not see it in terms of offices and riots, but of creative, constructive work, beginning at home.

Night and Day is a well-constructed novel, but a shade too deliberate, too obviously something that the author has made herself do. It has been greatly praised[22] for the good writing it contains. But I find the real interest to lie in the fact that it conveys the atmosphere of security and culture in the respectable middle-class intellectual family of pre-war London and describes the gradual change into a disintegrating society where the younger generation begins to move their own way. It is also an illuminating piece of work in another respect: besides glimpses of social satire, there is plenty of self-irony. It seems as if Virginia Woolf were in a state of transition herself, together with the age. She is trying to conform to something that is alien to her art and feels that she is a coward in not being herself. She feels both disappointed and satirical towards herself and her kind. No great merit, she finds, is required to be a Virginia Stephen. Once you bear a well-known name, nothing very much is required »to put you into a position where it is easier on the whole to be eminent than obscure. And if this is true of the sons, even the daughters, even in the nineteenth century, are apt to become people of importance — philanthropists and educationalists if they are spinsters, and the wives of distinguished men if they marry ... On the whole, in these first years of the twentieth century, the Alardyces and their relations were keeping their heads well above water. One finds them at the tops of professions, with letters after their names; they sit in luxurious public offices, with private secretaries attached to them; they write solid books in dark covers, issued by the presses of the two universities, and when one of them dies the chances are that another of them writes his biography.»[23] Virginia did obviously not intend to be satisfied with being »one of the Alardyces». She had a craving to be Virginia Woolf.

---

[22] for instance by Desmond MacCarthy (cf. *Criticism*, p. 173) and Edwin Muir who — rather surprisingly — finds it in many ways the finest of VW's novels; vide *Transition*, p. 72.

[23] *Night and Day*, pp. 30—31

VII

Virginia Woolf Finds Herself

»If a writer», Virginia Woolf had written in *Modern Fiction*, »if a writer were a free man and not a slave, if he could write what he chose, not what he must, if he could base his work upon his own feeling and not upon convention, there would be no plot, no comedy, no tragedy, no love interest or catastrophe in the accepted style, and perhaps not a single button sewn on as the Bond Street tailors would have it».[1] After *Night and Day* Virginia Woolf chose to be 'a free man'. By 1919 she was finished with the conventional method of writing. The short impressionistic sketches, *Kew Gardens*, *The Mark on the Wall*, and *Monday and Tuesday*, which T. S. Eliot called »the most curious and interesting example of a process of dissociation which in that direction — — cannot be exceeded»,[2] were the inauguration of a new era in her development as a writer. The only freedom we have is to apprehend life in our own peculiarly seen combinations, to work out our own salvation in our search for reality and truth. But to an extent even this freedom is tied up with the other factors in our life. For an artist, a Virginia Woolf herself, is a no-man's-land between the forces that have moulded her: heredity and environment on the one hand, and on the other the audience and the Zeitgeist with which she is either on rebellious or on friendly terms; in any case the influence is there, at work. Yet even if the artist is only a bubble in a stream with deep unseen undercurrents, the bubble has its own iridescence; light is refracted

---

[1] *The Common Reader* I, p. 189
[2] *The Dial*, Aug. 1921, LXXI, No. 2, p. 217

against it at a given moment differently from the neighbouring bubble. Always bearing in mind the existence of the artist's ultimate individuality, it is yet of interest to cast a look at Virginia Woolf's nearest surroundings. What was Bloomsbury doing round 1920?

As Bloomsbury was one of the avant-gardes of the intellectual achievement in England, new ideas were sure to have an airing in the informal gatherings on Thursday evenings. Round the time Virfinia Woolf was preparing *Jacob's Room*, her husband was engaged in translating, together with S. S. Koteliansky, *The Notebooks of Anton Tchekhov* (1921) and *The Autobiography of Countess Sophie Tolstoy* (1922). Virginia Woolf herself, also in collaboration with Koteliansky, translated *Stavrogin's Confessions* by Dostoevsky (1922), *Tolstoi's Love Letters* and *Talks with Tolstoi* (1923).[3] Lytton Strachey's *Eminent Victorians* (1918) and *Queen Victoria* (1921) had made a new way of writing biography popular. E. M. Forster had published *The Story of a Siren* in 1920, his guidebook to Alexandria in 1922, *Pharos and Pharillon* 1923, and was preparing his *Passage to India* (1924). Clive Bell's *Since Cézanne* appeared in 1922, Roger Fry's *Cézanne* was begun in 1924, though not published till 1927. His *Vision and Design* appeared in 1920. Maynard Keynes had published his *Economic Consequences of the Peace* in 1919. Bertrand Russell, with his customary and dangerous facility, spouted books and pamphlets by the dozen: *Mysticism and Logic* (1918), *The Analysis of Mind* (1921), *Free Thought and Propaganda* (1922), *The ABC of Atoms* (1923), *The ABC of Relativity* (1925). In 1914 he had written a treatise on the philosophy of Bergson, who had been the subject of several other English studies between 1915—1920. Virginia Woolf's sister-in-law, Karen Stephen, published an elucidation of Bergson's philosophy in 1922. In the same year The Hogarth Press began the publication of the International Psycho-Analytical Library, and from that year on, till his death, translations of all Freud's works were published by The Hogarth Press, i.e. Leonard

---

[3] The English had been made aware of the mastery of the Russian authors by Constance Garnett's translations which started in 1912.

and Virginia Woolf. Jung's *Psychology of the Unconscious* had been translated in 1918, *Psychological Types* in 1923, Adler's *Practice and Theory of Individual Psychology* in 1924. Joyce's *Ulysses* was appearing in *The Little Review* in 1919 and was given favourable attention in Virginia Woolf's essay on *Modern Fiction*. T. S. Eliot's *Prufrock* in 1917 had drawn intelligent readers towards the new poet; his *Waste Land* was published by The Hogarth Press in 1923. Aldous Huxley's *Chrome Yellow* had appeared in 1921. Proust's *Swann's Way*, the first part of *A la Recherche du Temps Perdu*, was translated into English in 1922. A great deal of discussion must have gone on around him, though Clive Bell's *Proust* did not come out till 1928.

Though influences are not in themselves overwhelmingly important — it is what the recipient makes of them that matters — it remains of interest to see how the atmosphere around Virginia Woolf was steeped with new ideas. They were bound to affect her alert, receptive, and questioning mind, because they happened to be the kind of ideas that would especially appeal to her. Psychoanalysis gave her added interest in the subconscious and helped her to decide on the choice of the inner monologue. Bergson, with his theories of intuition, élan vital, and constant change, was congenial to her own bent of mind and ideas of time-continuum. She felt, for all her Bloomsburyism, strong attraction towards the philosophical theories which reacted against purely intellectual analysis of the universe. Before General Smuts' Holism became formulated[4] or Koffka's *Principles of Gestalt Psychology* was published (1935), Virginia Woolf seems to have been inclined to see the universe in terms of organic wholes. She is always after a 'pattern', a design of which the human mind may form a part.[5]

Virginia Woolf's attitude to the Russian authors was one of both attraction and repulsion. Gilbert H. Phelps, in his study on the subject,[6] has drawn attention to some similarities in them, to fear, for instance, which he finds a common feature to both, or to fierce

---

[4] *Holism and Evolution* appeared in 1926.
[5] cf. abodve p. 88, note 18
[6] *Cambridge Review*, 17. 10. 42, Vol. LXIV No. 1556, pp. 21 ff.

questioning which tends to destroy outward serenity. Those qualities are, however, so thoroughly part and parcel of Virginia Woolf's mental make-up that it is difficult to believe that they are due to any outward influence. Her fear and questioning are individual traits, grown up from the soil of personal experiences and weak nerves. The constant, almost masochistic search for the 'soul', characteristic of the Russians, is , as Virginia Woolf points out in her essay on *The Russian Point of View*,[7] something unspeakably alien and looked upon with mistrust — and sometimes with fascination — by the empirical, level-headed English. There is something absolute in the Russian approach to themselves and the universe; the traditional English attitude is one of compromise: they would like to have their cake and eat it. Another comparison Virginia Woolf draws in her essay is also relevant to our study: the different structures of society. The barrier between individuals and classes does not play as great a role in Russia as it does in England where society, to quote the above-mentioned essay, »is sorted out into lower and upper classes, each with its own traditions, its own manners, and, to some extent, its own language. Whether he wishes or not, there is a constant pressure upon an English novelist to recognize these barriers, and, in consequence, order is imposed on him and some kind of form; he is inclined to satire rather than to compassion, to scrutiny of society rather than understanding of individuals themselves.»[8] Virginia Woolf is always conscious of, and interested in, society, the potential audience of what the writer has to say; she accepts the hedging off of the different groups of people. This attitude reflects itself in her essays especially, but also in her whole relation to audience.

We can say with some safety that the main characteristic of the English novel has been, and still is, its middle-classness: written by middle-class authors for a middle-class public, it has taken up a self-imposed role of being a protector of social virtues, hence its tendency

---

[7] *The Common Reader* I, pp. 219 ff.
[8] ibid., p. 228

to moralize. That, at any rate, is the great tradition handed down by Richardson, Sterne, and Smollett to the Victorians and further to the Edwardians and Georgians, down to the latest representatives, the Graham Greenes and Evelyn Waughs who are constantly preoccupied with the sense of guilt and atonement. At first glance Virginia Woolf does not quite fit in with the tradition. She is not a moralist in the obvious sense; no true artist is.[9] In her, ethics become assimilated with aesthetics in the Bloomsbury manner: good states of mind are the highest good for her too. But it implies the sense of values; insofar she is a moralist. The diversity and width of the modern reading public make it far more difficult for a writer to reach everybody than it was, let us say, in Dickens's days. It becomes downright impossible if you are, like Virginia Woolf, first of all a metaphysical aesthete, and, secondly, choose to write in the form of prose-poetry. The bulk of the audience are shy of any mental effort. They are like the listeners to the Light Programme of the BBC, passive receivers of easy entertainment. It is — to keep to the simile — the audience of the Third Programme that Virginia Woolf deliberately chose to address — those willing to make a conscious effort in listening, to use their minds actively, or to attune themselves to acceptance of her lyrical mood. It has been said [10] that her choice was that of an egoist, an excuse for remaining in her study. But in that very wide sense every artist is an egoist, for is not rendering one's own experience the primary artistic concern which in a work of art becomes a social act; hunting for generalized truths and transcendental meanings is only a sequence. Virginia Woolf aimed at both. Particular truths, in that age of disillusionment, were the only ones she could with reliance lay her hands on, but she was always after large general patterns within the framework of her own limited experience. However, when it came to a choice between sacrificing either the width of communication between the author and the public, or the quality of her experience, then quality of experience must come first. It was there that she asserted her freedom.

[9] cf. Thomas Mann in *The Listener*, June 5, 1952, pp. 911 ff.
[10] Daiches: *The Novel and the Modern World*, p. 182

In public opinion as well as in the opinion of most critics Virginia Woolf is a typical ivory-tower writer, separated from the realities of life by her voluntary retirment into the realm of an aesthete, and of a feminine aesthete at that. William Troy has aptly called her world »a superior Bohemia».[11] It is a limited area, but not so limited nor so ivory as some critics, especially on the other side of the Atlantic, would like us to believe.[12]

---

[11] *Lit..Opinion in America*, p. 342

[12] A short survey to the recent trends in Virginia Woolf-criticism may be to the point. The earliest longer studies, those by Winifred Holtby and Floris Delattre, both in the same year, 1932, depicting Virginia Woolf more »in the round» than most of the later critics, are both works still worth consulting. Joan Bennett, of Cambridge, in her conscientious and reverent study, keeps to a narrower field, to the analysis of VW's art. R. L. Chambers offers interesting criticism and comparisons with the contemporary world. Deborah Newton's slender book is too much limited to giving an account of the works to compete with the others in importance. Quite the most illuminating of the recent books is Bernard Blackstone's thorough and intelligent interpretation of VW's 'message' (1949). For him, VW becomes pre-eminently a philosophical writer. He brings out VW the mystic. — It is not surprising to see that women have been particularly attracted towards studying one of the most feminine of all writers. Ruth Gruber's is the most interesting, being less technical in its approach than the other German treatises (Badenhausen, I, *Die Sprache VWs*, 1932; Finke, Ilse, *VWs Stellung zur Wirklichkeit*, 1953; Lohmüller, Gertrude, *Die Frau im Werk von VW*, 1937; Weidner, E. F., *Impressionismus und Expressionismus in den Romanen VWs*, 1934) Nationality is no bar. Among the critics who have written more extensive studies of VW there are American, Argentine, Australian, English, French, Finnish, German, Spanish and Swedish names. Actually it can be said that at the moment her fame is greater abroad — at least on the continent — than in Britain.

The shorter studies are too numerous to be mentioned here. Not all deserve a special mention, either. E. M. Forster's Rede Lecture on VW naturally rouses expectations, but as it was a memorial lecture delivered soon after the author's death, he refrained from any deeper critical assessment of her either as an artist or as a personality. In his earlier essay (included in *Abinger Harvest*, pp. 104—112) he speaks of 'elusiveness' as the most characteristic feature of VW's early novels. Of the English essays on VW, besides those mentioned in other connections above or below, it may suffice to mention those by Elizabeth

Some of her defenders argue justly that although Virginia Woolf refused to deal with life in the surface manner of a popular novelist and decided to concentrate on the relation between art and life, her choice cannot be called that of an escapist, for she was constantly

---

Drew in *The Modern Novel*, 1926, and by Dorothy Hoare in *Some Studies in the Modern Novel*, 1938.

VW's American critics have all along been irritated by her, in their opinion, extreme aestheticism, and have been concerned with her from the social point of view rather than from the artistic angle, placing their object of criticism in a wider context. David Daiches, (now Lecturer in English Lit., Cambridge Univ.) whose *Virginia Woolf* has been written with all possible objectivity and insight, gives this species the rather clumsy name of »maximum-context criticism» in his *Novel and the Modern World*, 1938, p. 213. It is applied, e.g., by William Troy in *Literary Opinion in America*, 1937, reprinted from the *Symposium*, Jan. and Apr., 1932; by Herbert J. Muller in *Modern Fiction*, 1937; Elizabeth Monroe in *The Novel and Society*, 1941 (vide esp. ch. *Experimental Humanism in Virginia Woolf*, pp. 188 ff.), to mention only some that have treated the subject in greater detail. Having mainly been aestheticising or explanatory, the more recent British criticism of Virginia Woolf has begun to speak very much in the same tone as the earlier American variety. Not that it has ever lacked a critical vein — we need only read articles in *Scrutiny* by the Leavises, or D. S. Savage on Bloomsbury in *The Withered Branch* to find a Swinnerton quite mild in comparison: off fly both Virginia Woolf and E. M. Forster into the dustbin. But lately even 'Bloomsbury-minded' critics, like Lord David Cecil and Elizabeth Bowen, (though sympathetic in her essay in *Collected Impressions*, pp. 79 ff.) have begun looking at Virginia Woolf from what we might call a moralist's angle. Lord David Cecil goes the whole hog and declares Virginia Woolf's novels to be »without drama, without moral values, and without character or strong personal emotion». (*Poets and Story-Tellers*, p. 170). But to work on a novel, consciously planned to be devoid of those elements, must be as difficult as conjuring a rabbit out of an empty hat. The critic does not deny the difficulty; all the same his final judgement is a rather questionable praise: he finds it a relief »for once in a way, freed from the claims of heart and conscience, to concentrate on the mere spectacle of a world so brimful of strangeness and fascination and delight! How cleansing to be transported, if only for an hour, to a region where it is more important to be clever than to be good, and more important to be beautiful than to be either!» (ibid., p. 180). But is it really fair to Virginia Woolf?

occupied with the sense of values which made her a humanist.[13] The underdog, as also Elizabeth Bowen points out,[14] was not forgotten in Virginia Woolf's novels. Although she did not make it her job to write about social injustices — apart from her femininist activities — and of the existence of the lower levels of consciousness, she was acutely, though somewhat *ex cathedra*, aware of them and her sympathy was always with those who suffer. With her mind she, like Mrs. Ramsay, »had always seized the fact that there is no reason, order, justice: but suffering, death, the poor. There was no treachery too base for the world to commit; she knew that. No happiness lasted; she knew that.»[15] »When I am with artists», she makes Mrs. Dalloway say in *The Voyage Out*, »I feel so intensely the delights of shutting oneself up in a little world of one's own, with pictures and music and everything beautiful, and then I go out in the streets and the first child I meet with its poor, hungry, dirty little face makes me turn round and say, 'No, I can't shut myself up — I won't live in a world of my own. I should like to stop all the painting and writing and music until this kind of thing exists no longer.' Don't you feel — that life is a perpetual conflict?»[16] In Mrs. Dalloway's mouth the words may sound an empty phrase of a snob, but Virginia Woolf herself was really painfully conscious of the conflict, the more so because she was »at one remove», to use Elizabeth Bowen's words.[17] As an artist, however, she had to make a choice in her material, for her method imposed on her a need of fierce selection. She had to be drastic in her exclusions. For her, the world resembled the opera with its system of classification: stalls, boxes, amphitheatre, gallery. »The moulds are filling nightly. There is no need to distinguish details. But the difficulty remains — one has to choose. — — Never was there a harsher necessity! or one which entails greater pain,

---

[13] cf. Blackstone: *Virginia Woolf*, pp. 159—260
[14] op. cit., p. 82
[15] *To the Lighthouse*, p. 102
[16] *The Voyage Out*, p. 45
[17] op. cit., p. 81

more certain disaster; for wherever I seat myself, I die in exile — —.»[18] Her choice was for the stalls, the middle-classes and the workings of their minds. Knowing perhaps her limitations, she concentrated on what she knew best and could penetrate most successfully. Who can blame her? The mind, of, say, a charwoman was more alien to her than that of one who belonged to her own class, who shared her interests and cultural background. As she was expressly occupied with the mind, she had to leave a large class of people alone and concentrate on her particular field. But she did not lack sympathy — she »died in exile» — towards those whose life was spent in manual action instead of mental, who are — whatever their class — practical members of society, not solitary contemplatives. When Mrs. Mop sees a mark on the wall, her instincts urge her towards action. When Virginia Woolf and her like see the same thing, it starts a whole chain of thoughts and images in their minds culminating perhaps in metaphysical speculations, in the realization of the »mystery of life! The inaccuracy of thought! The ignorance of humanity!»[19] Mrs. Mop would, instead, walk towards the wall to see what the mark is, and having seen that it is a snail do something about it. No, describing her would not have been suitable material for what Virginia Woolf had in mind to do. Mrs. Mop could not be drawn with hints and implications; she is not complex enough. Virginia Woolf decided to keep to her own kind.

After having tried her hand at three impressionistic sketches, Virginia Woolf now embarked on a more extensive attempt at what was to become the typical — if there is such a thing — Virginia Woolf-method of writing. The theory she had expressed in *Modern Fiction* was being put into practice for the first time. »No plot, no comedy, no tragedy, no love interest or catastrophe in the accepted style», she had said. »Life is not a series of gig lamps symmetrically arranged; life is a luminous halo, a semi-transparent envelope

---

[18] *Jacob's Room*, pp. 67—68
[19] *The Mark on the Wall* in *Haunted House*, p. 36

surrounding us from the beginning of consciousness to the end. Is it not», Virginia Woolf asks, »the task of the novelist to convey this varying, this unknown and uncircumscribed spirit, whatever aberration or complexity it may display, with as little mixture of the alien and external as possible?»[20] In the essay *Mr. Bennett and Mrs. Brown* the latter represented 'Mrs Brownness', i.e. the spirit of life which Virginia tried to catch in her novels. In life no one sees anyone as he really is, she claims. It is only by snatches that we can grasp the reality of another person. »It seems», the author says in *Jacob's Room*, her next novel, »that a profound, impartial, and absolutely just opinion of our fellow-creatures is utterly unknown. — — In any case life is but a procession of shadows, and God knows why it is that we embrace them so eagerly and see them depart with such anguish, being shadows. And why, if this and much more than this is true, why are we yet surprised in the window corner by a sudden vision that the young man in the chair is of things in the world the most real, the most solid, the best known to us — why indeed? For the moment after we know nothing about him. Such is the manner of our seeing. Such the condition of our love.»[21] Consequently, it is not Jacob that Virginia Woolf is trying to build up by hints and allusions, it is 'Jacobness', the elusive spirit of life.

Virginia Woolf did not lose any of her nearest relatives in the war, but the thought of the numerous young men who never returned must have brought back vividly the memory of Thoby Stephen who had some ten years earlier (1905) paid a visit to Greece and died soon after. A young man, glowing with life, had vanished. Nothing was left of him but his room, some letters, writings, and clothes. What had he been like? Could he be reconstrued from the reflections of the impact he had left on other people's minds? Is that not, perhaps after all, the truest picture of a human being, Virginia Woolf seemed to have asked herself. *Jacob's Room* is her answer. It is an experimental attempt, rather reminding the reader of Bertrand Russell's

---

[20] *The Common Reader* I, p. 189
[21] *Jacob's Room*, p. 71

theory that man is nothing but a series of distinct and separate events, to create character by the cinematographic flash-back technique which has since become so popular. The consecutive story is abandoned; the scene keeps on shifting from one place to another: Cornwall, Cambridge, London, Paris, Athens, flash on the screen in disrupted glimpses. The focus is now on someone's mind, now on a chain of events, but never long on any one centre. Jacob Flanders, when we first meet him, is an imaginative little boy of the type for whom a sheep's skull, found on the shore of the Cornish coast, is full of mystery. He grows up into an awkward, rather silent young man who has a tendency to find »loveliness infernally sad»[22] yet at the same time having »the seeds of extreme disillusionment»[23] in him. He is »unwordly»[24] in the sense Bloomsbury was fond of applying the epithet to themselves in their Cambridge days: success, money, position mean very little to him. Jacob comes up to Cambridge in 1906, is inevitably moulded into a lover of Greek civilization, and enjoys the delights of intimacy, »a sort of suppleness, when mind prints upon mind indelibly».[25] With the description of Jacob's development we are shifted into a definite cultural atmosphere, that of the Cambridge which moulded Bloomsbury. The book is at least as much an attempt to evoke a Stimmung as to draw a character — the atmosphere of Bloomsbury at its most youthful and unspoilt. It is more the Cambridge of G. L. Dickinson, E. M. Forster, and Leonard Woolf than that of the 'irreverent' Lytton Strachey. Virginia Woolf shares, at least partly, her friends' nostalgia for the lights of Cambridge — »Greek burns there; science there; philosophy on the ground floor. — — So that if at night, far out at sea over the tumbling waves, one saw a haze on the waters, a city illuminated, a whiteness even in the sky, such as that now over the Hall of Trinity where they're still dining, or washing up plates, that would be the

---

[22] ibid., p. 47
[23] ibid., p. 158
[24] cf. Keynes' *Two Memoirs*, p. 84
[25] *Jacob's Room*, p. 44

light burning there — the light of Cambridge.»[26] Tradition, friends, beauty were the inheritance, and Jacob carries it wherever he goes. Lines of Virgil and Lucretius float in his mind even in the tumult of London traffic. »The enormous mind»[27] stocked on the shelves of the British Museum is a constant source of respectful amazement to him. After leaving the University, Jacob leads the life of a young, tolerably well-off, middle-class intellectual, trying his hand at writing. His trip to Greece reveals to him her beauty, but also her tragedy, »the tragedy of all high souls. The inevitable compromise.»[28]

Sympathetic though the author is towards the Cambridge products of culture, she is not wholly blind to their weaknesses. She is still the same critical sister who would visit her brothers in Cambridge and smilingly listen to their incessant talk, in which she detected plenty of arrogance and superiority. »It is not simple, or pure, or wholly splendid, the lamp of learning, since if you see them under its light (whether Rossetti's on the wall, or Van Gogh reproduced, whether there are lilacs in the bowl or rusty pipes), how priestly they look! How like a suburb where you go to see a view and eat a special cake! Back you go to London, for the treat is over.»[29] The long talks in the undergraduates' rooms make her only feel amused, not infuriated like D. H. Lawrence who, having met the set in Russell's rooms in Trinity College, contracted a violent dislike towards them. But, then, Lawrence never did anything by halves. »To hear these young people talk», he writes to Lady Ottoline Morrell, »really fills me with black fury: they talk endlessly, but endlessly — and never, never a good thing said. They are cased each in a hard little shell of his own and out of this they talk words. There is never for one second, any outgoing of feeling and no reverence, not a crumb or grain of reverence. I cannot stand it. I will not have people like this — I rather be alone. They made me dream of

---

[26] ibid., p. 38
[27] ibid., p. 40
[28] ibid., p. 141
[29] ibid., p. 38

a beetle that bites like a scorpion — —».[30] In D. H. Lawrence and Bloomsbury two worlds stood opposite. On one side stood that privileged world of comfort and culture represented by our young rebels whose fine sensibilities were being sunned under the rays of the same Victorian ultra-violet lamp that they were so anxious to smash. It was a limited world, a hothouse, compared with that of D. H. Lawrence, the world of poverty, struggle, and emotional inhibitions, but of close touch with other human beings. Keynes hints at Lawrence's jealousy. There may have been (very probably was) class-resentment in him, for being a miner's son, even a talented son, was a handicap and a brand of astonishing depth in Britain — or perhaps one should here say England and exempt the other parts of the United Kingdom. Lawrence was driven by his daimon; what he was, he had to be, there was no alternative. Compared with his burning intensity, the play-boy quality of the young Lytton Stracheys and Clive Bells stands to their disadvantage, and their cultivation of 'states of mind' which only involved 'being good', not 'doing good', seems nauseously irresponsible. They aspire to be the English variety of the Encyclopédistes — »to dispel the dark mass of superstition, ignorance, and folly by the clear rays of truth»;[31] their jargon was an imitation of the Gallic »mingling of gaiety, irony and common sense».[32] But their French examples did not teach them how to avoid their mistakes, and so, what Lytton Strachey says of the philosophers of the 18th century applies, word for word, to himself and his set: »The lack», he says, »of psychological insight which was so common in the eighteenth century tended to narrow their sympathies; and in particular they failed to realize the beauty and significance of religious and mystical states of mind. These defects eventually produced a reaction against their teaching — a reaction during which the true value of their work was for a time obscured.»[33] It reads

---

[30] quoted in David Garnett's Introductory Note to *My Early Beliefs* in Keynes' *Two Memoirs*, p. 76

[31] Lytton Strachey: *Landmarks*, p. 87

[32] idem

[33] ibid., pp. 96—97

exactly like present-day criticism of Bloomsbury, in fact like Lord Keynes' criticism of himself and his friends, included in his *Two Memoirs*, published in 1949, but written as early as 1938. Lawrence, with his mysticism and belief in the deep underlying passions and in the irrationality of the human nature, seems to have had deeper understanding towards his fellow-creatures than Bloomsbury with their belief in the ultimate omnipotence of reason. In Lawrence's days Bloomsbury were still at their most arrogant and irreverent. In Lord Keynes' *Memoirs* the reader gets a glimpse of them at their best: endearingly self-critical, deeply concerned about mankind, mellowly mature.

E. M. Forster and Virginia Woolf were never quite as great believers in the progress of human rationality as the others. There is in both a strain of mysticism. Human passions and irrelevances play a considerable role in E. M. Forster's books, and Virginia Woolf shows time and again how little reason helps us to interpret other human beings and how greatly we are at the mercy of our impulses. »The streets of London have their maps; but our passions are uncharted», she says in *Jacob's Room*.[34] No one knows what is round the corner. Jacob's maturing in mind and body progressed through the customary trial and error stages. He turned a corner, and there was death waiting for him. Betty Flanders, his mother, hears the guns on the other side of the Channel »as if nocturnal women were beating large carpets»,[35] one of the author's happy 'shock' images. Jacob does not return from the war. But he continues to live in his friends' memories and, perhaps, in places he had loved. That is all that is left of Jacob. And that is all Virginia Woolf ventures to say about immortality, either at this stage or later.

---

[34] p. 94
[35] p. 175

VIII

Mrs. Dalloway

The element of fear, referred to in connection with the possible Russian influence,[1] is a characteristic which deserves closer consideration. For Virginia Woolf, fear is in human life as important a factor — a highly negative one — as love, which is positive. Fear it is that separates people from each other, fear of being laughed at, giving themselves away, of thinking differently from other people. On top of those daily little fears is the big, looming, ubiquitous fear: the fear of death. The goodness and safety of life are only on the surface; nothing has a chance against death. In fact Virginia Woolf's novels are constructed around death just as much as around life. *Night and Day* is the only one where it does not play any part. In *Between the Acts* it is not mentioned but, instead, the whole atmosphere is that before a storm; unnatural stillness, ominous expectance, melancholy flashbacks into the happier past prophesy the approach of a tornado which will uproot houses and trees, swallow ships into its spiral shape.

Virginia Woolf's own vessel was moored at an insecure quay. Not only was the sea stormy, but the moorings were loose. A daughter of a sworn agnostic, she had been taught to do without religion, to be satisfied with a belief that, as Rachel says in *The Voyage Out*, »there are things we don't know about, and the world might change in a minute and anything appear».[2] Virginia Woolf remained in a state of suspense, full of anticipation and query, but none of her metaphysical questions ever got an answer, none reached a stage of strong,

---

[1] cf. above pp. 93 ff.
[2] p. 168

positive conviction. They remained 'matches struck in the dark'. Leslie Stephen had struggled for his agnostic's faith, it was therefore something positive, a real conviction. His daughter was brought up an agnostic, she had made no sacrifices for her belief, therefore it was more an unbelief than a belief. Like all Bloomsbury, she had an almost hostile attitude towards doctrinal religion. It is presented in her novels as a bogey, threatening people's liberty, warping their vision. Its representatives are shown as a positive menace to the happiness of mankind: a stupid, preaching headmaster of a school,[3] or a sadistic, frustrated spinster[4] who uses God for her own unpleasant purposes. Mrs. Woolf's husband was equally strongly anti-religious as can be seen from his *After the Deluge I* and other writings. But in Virginia Woolf there was development towards a more balanced view. Mrs. Swithin, in *Between the Acts*, is a likeable figure in all her childlikeness. Her trustful resorts to prayers and her constant fingering of the golden cross are presented without irony. But, then, her religion is not orthodox, but presented as melting into a kind of pantheism, »one-making», as the author calls it. »Sheep, cows, grass, trees, ourselves — all are one. If discordant, producing harmony — if not to us, to a gigantic ear attached to a gigantic head. And thus — — the agony of the particular sheep, cow, or human being, is necessary; and so — — we reach the conclusion that all is harmony, could we hear it. And we shall.»[5] [6]

Virginia Woolf felt the insecurity of life with a greater acuteness than most people. The experiences of her childhood, her unstable nerves of which she never knew when they would give way,[7] all

---

[3] in *The Waves*, p. 37

[4] Miss Kilman in *Mrs. Dalloway*

[5] *Between the Acts*, p. 204

[6] Other instances of the author's pantheistic attitude are to be found all over her work. Cf. *Orlando*, p. 285, *The Waves*, pp. 41—42, 245; *The Years*, pp. 461—2; *Evening over Sussex* in *The Death of the Moth*, p. 13

[7] She had had a complete mental breakdown after her mother's death and tried to commit a suicide. Another breakdown took place ab. 1903 when she had to stay in the country a year or two; in 1914—15 again a complete breakdown with an attempt of a suicide took place.

acting on her abnormal sensitivity did their share in heightening the feeling. As she could not believe in a personal God, she had to find a substitute — for it seems that however much people are convinced that they can do without metaphysics, on a closer examination it appears that they, if not religious, take up the cult of aestheticism, political dogmas, humanism; the craving for a kind of metaphysical thinking is there, at work. Hence also, it would seem, Virginia Woolf's constant hankering after large patterns in the universe, her pantheistic conception of life, tireless pre-occupation with questions of metaphysical content, her belief — for all her rationalism — in the transcendental purpose of life which, as such, already presupposes some kind of God, even if not the God of Wrath and Eternal Damnation. Humanism and aestheticism seemed to be enough for most of her friends; not quite enough for her. She was far from being a full-fledged rationalist or a true sceptic who adamantly refuses to believe in theories which are not watertight when intellectual criticism is applied to them. There is a strong resemblance — stronger than she would have liked to admit — between her metaphysical thought and that of McTaggart and Lowes Dickinson.

Mrs. Dalloway is the mouthpiece of Virginia Woolf's transcendental theory, such as it is, »which, with her horror of death, allowed her to believe, or say that she believed (for all her scepticism), that since our apparitions, the part of us which appears, are so momentary compared with the other, the unseen part of us, which spreads wide, the unseen might survive, be recovered somehow attached to this person or that, or even haunting certain places, after death. Perhaps — perhaps.»[8] It is practically what Virginia Woolf had said in *Jacob's Room*, and what she will go on saying till the end of her days: some kind of pantheism remained for her a substitute for orthodox religion. Its adequacy, however, remains an open question judging from the lack of synthesis in her works and the sense of futility that she is unable to dispel. Virginia Woolf was a questioner, not a giver of answers. But she was asking such difficult

---

[8] *Mrs. Dalloway*, p. 168

questions that giving an answer is not always possible. Asking the right questions, however, may be more important than trying to answer them: my answer in these difficult problems may not be that of my neighbour.

»Let us not take it for granted», Virginia Woolf had said in *Modern Fiction*, »that life exists more fully in what is commonly thought big than in what is commonly thought small».[9] It is characteristic of her love of combining seeming trivialities with things of momentous importance that she turns Clarissa Dalloway, the superficial snob, the fashionable London hostess, into her mouthpiece in matters of life and death; that she illuminates her transcendental theory through the ruminations of one who, on the surface, would seem to be the last person to give much time to serious thinking. But, Virginia Woolf constantly reminds us, one must not take things at their face value. One of her recurrent themes is the unexpectedness of human nature. No two persons could be farther apart from each other than Clarissa Dalloway and Septimus Warren Smith, the shell-shocked ex-soldier who speaks to his dead friend and hears the sparrow in Regent's Park »sing freshly and piercingly in Greek words how there is no crime and, joined by another sparrow, they sang in voices prolonged and piercing in Greek words, from trees in the meadow of life beyond the river where the dead walk, how there is no death».[10] Yet those two are in many ways identical, because they are contrapunctal melodies of the same theme, and the theme is Virginia Woolf herself; she invests almost all her characters with her own vision. She herself might hear — probably heard when the delusions of a nervous breakdown began to attack her; she had just recovered from one when she started *Mrs. Dalloway* — the sparrows sing in Greek; but it is most unlikely that a Septimus Warren Smith's sparrows would sing in Greek.[11] Here we spot one of Virginia Woolf's

---

[9] *The Common Reader* I, p. 190

[10] *Mrs. Dalloway*, p. 28

[11] An illuminating account of a lunatic's strange world of images and hallucinations, very much the same as that of Septimus, appeared in *The Listener*, Apr. 10, 1952, pp. 150 ff.

weaknesses as a novelist: she cannot often enough resist the temptation not to leave her characters alone, to be themselves. They have a tendency to be Virginia Woolf. Rachel and Katherine, Clarissa and Septimus, Orlando, all the characters in *The Waves*, are looking at the world with the eyes of their creator, and although they are wise and discerning eyes, their range of vision is of necessity limited. *Mrs. Dalloway*, in its innermost content, is in a particularly large measure about the author herself. With Clarissa she pre-lives the agonies of death, with Septimus she re-lives the ordeal of losing her reason, of which she had had recent personal experience. Considering that, there cannot be said to be any maudlin sentimentality in the book, on the contrary. The step from *Jacob's Room* is a great advance in the maturity of feeling. The reader gets the impression that the author has fought an uneven battle with the fate from which she has emerged a victor, full of wisdom and love and with a conviction that the unfathomable mystery of life and death might be solved somehow, sometime. In the light of what happened some 16 years later such a passage as the following gains illuminating importance. Virginia Woolf had, one feels, learned how to practice the art of dying so that, when the moment came on March 28, 1941, she only repeated what she had already done many times before. »So on a summer's day,» she wrote in 1925, »waves collect, overbalance, and fall; collect and fall; and the whole world seems to be saying 'that is all' more and more ponderously, until even the heart in the body which lies in the sun on the beach says too, that is all. Fear no more, says the heart. Fear no more, says the heart, committing its burden to some sea, which sighs collectively for all sorrows, and renews, begins, collects, lets fall. And the body alone listens to the passing bee; the wave breaking; the dog barking, far away barking and barking.»[12] Ripeness is all.

There is no way out of the dilemma for Septimus either, except through suicide. Clarissa's life is on the surface full of delightful things, love, money, parties, laughter, safety. Yet she too feels the

---

[12] ibid., pp. 44—45

insecurity of life, the perishableness of beauty, the anguish behind the laughter. Here is a parallel case to that of Septimus. Middle-aged, she feels her life dwindle away, the margin of existence become incapable of stretching any further. »Narrower and narrower would her bed be.»[13] In all her shallowness Clarissa is aware of greater issues in life and feels painfully her own incapacity of 'making figures'. Death is for her, too, the only solution of the problem; she identifies herself with Septimus when she hears of this unknown man's suicide.[14] »Death was defiance», she felt. »Death was an attempt to communicate, people feeling the impossibility of reaching the centre which, mystically, evaded them; closeness drew apart; rapture faded; one was alone. There was embrace in death.»[15]

All Virginia Woolf's books are sprinkled with wonderful descriptions of the love of life and with innumerable definitions of what life is. She tries to imprison in her words life's momentousness, its elusiveness, its incongruity, its order and pattern, its horror and loveliness. She feels exalted and carried away with the exquisite states of mind that life produces in her. But her approach takes mostly place, not on the every-day level of senses, but on that of sensibilities; the passion, the vehemence, and the warmth of real life are closed out. The embrace is in death, she herself says. The impression is created that Virginia Woolf was, after all, not really on the side of life, as she declared to be; hence, perhaps, partly the sense of futility. She refined life till it slipped through her fingers. The air of her world is light Alpine air, easy to breathe, exhilarating. But at the same time one misses the vigorousness of reality, as if one were lying in a sanatorium up in the mountains, a patient with an abnormally heightened consciousness and feeling of lightness, caused by a slight rise in temperature, exalted, but not quite of this world.

---

[13] ibid., p. 35

[14] In the earliest draft of the novel there was no Septimus; it was Clarissa who killed herself.

[15] ibid., p. 202

The inner monologue has in *Mrs. Dalloway* found an expression as satisfactory as in any English work of art. Some technical artificialities, like the recurrent boom of the Big Ben or the sound of a motor-tyre, have been deliberately installed to link up the pieces of the story, but in its content it runs smoothly and effortlessly.[16] Within the framework of one day we get the whole course of a human life, of several human lives, in fact.

The day of the story begins with Clarissa Dalloway's going to buy flowers for her party; it ends with that party. Within the time limit of one day we see several characters being built cleverly by means of glimpses and digressions. What is seemingly incongruous, becomes part of the pattern. What first strikes us as trivial, is shown to be important. Clarissa, the shallow, becomes the interpreter of a transcendental theory of life and death. Septimus, the insane, has the true conception of the meaning of truth and beauty. Sir William Bradshaw, the eminent nerve-specialist, becomes the embodiment of tyranny. Rezia, the inexperienced Italian girl, emanates protective love, warmth, and womanly tenderness. Peter Walsh, the good-for-nothing, has yet a deep understanding of life and human nature. Richard Dalloway, the successful politician, is at heart a shy youth, ready to worship and idolize. Everybody is slightly out of focus, like Mrs. Cameron's[17] photographs; the outlines are blurred, the images of human beings are made transparent so that their idea may shine through. *Mrs. Dalloway* was a great victory for Mrs. Woolf's technique in the conveying of her vision.

---

[16] cf. John Hawley Roberts in PMLA, Sept. 1946, Vol. LXI, No. 3, pp. 835—47, on the symbolism of formal devices in *Mrs. Dalloway*.

[17] vide the next chapter pp. 122 ff.

IX

To the Lighthouse

Mrs. Dalloway had been a study of a virginal, aloof, solitary character, who resents the absorption of passion as well as the shackles of love and feels happiest when least tied to another human being. *To the Lighthouse* presents in many ways a contrasting picture of a woman. Mrs. Ramsay is a born wife and mother with an unquenchable store of warmth and all-embracing tenderness. If an attic room and a narrow bed symbolize Mrs. Dalloway, a drawing-room and a nursery, full of life, laughter, and children's voices, reflect the atmosphere of Mrs. Ramsay's story. *To the Lighthouse* is pre-eminently about Mrs. Ramsay. She is the nucleus around which everything and everyone circulates, even the temperamental and egotistic Mr. Ramsay, in whom we have learnt — mutatis mutandis — to look for Leslie Stephen's features. Mrs. Ramsay's picture is also drawn from life, with the loving hand and nostalgic tenderness of one who was only in her teens when she lost her mother, the model of the picture. Yet the author does not let sentimental aspects mar the story which grows into a monument erected not only in honour of the author's mother, but in honour of the woman's 'good life' in general. Mrs. Ramsay is 'une âme bien née' in a truly Montaignesque sense. Her life, simple enough in outward circumstances, is rich in content and becomes moulded into a work of art by inward order and discipline.

All Virginia Woolf's books reflect the author, but none in a greater degree than *To the Lighthouse*. Dangerous though too much reading of an author into his work is, one is here tempted to surmise important revelation. Firstly, there is the autobiographical element; secondly, interesting illumination is thrown on the process of artistic creation, and, thirdly, the book grows into a treatise on the much-discussed theme of the 'good life', seen expressly from a woman's point of view. Thus the book not only sheds light on the author's growth of personality in the light of family relations and inheritance, but also on the work of her artist's imagination as well as on her ideas concerning values. It could thus be a key into her personality, into its most secret lockers even, if only one would find out how to use the combinations of the key.

To build up a picture of Virginia Woolf is still like trying to fit in pieces of a puzzle of which some may be missing and the picture therefore in danger of becoming distorted. The main facts of her life are known,[1] but her inner life is still hidden; no intimate letters or similar material are yet available. Still, a greater intimacy with her may not materially change the picture that can be based on her works. I should say[2] that Virginia Woolf was a very personal writer indeed; the mental atmosphere of her nearest surroundings was faithfully reflected in her works. Has she not, besides, said herself — »Every secret of a writer's soul, every experience of his life, every quality of his mind is written large in his works»?[3] Exaggerated, undoubtedly, but still not without truth in her own case! The writing is there, only do we know how to decipher it? And are we entitled to attempt a deciphering which must of necessaity remain based on conjectures?

In her essay on *How One Should Read a Book*,[4] Virginia Woolf herself touches this controversial question. How far is it safe to let the man interpret the writer? she asks, but does not commit herself to giving any answer. Obviously, in fact, no general answer can be

---

[1] Holtby, Delattre, and Daiches pay a fair amount of attention to the biographical details.

[2] contrary to Elizabeth Monroe, who is of the opinion (op. cit. p. 193) that Virginia Woolf's art is purely aesthetic, cut off from its social and spiritual environment.

[3] *Orlando*, pp. 189—190

[4] *The Common Reader* II, pp. 258—270

given. With a Shakespeare, very little is known about the personality behind the works, and what is known may seem immaterial and unnecessary for interpreting his art. On the other hand, the tortured souls of Dostoevsky become more understandable, perhaps gain new depth, if we look at them through the magnifying glass of their creator's life. A 'difficult' writer like Virginia Woolf herself may step nearer to the reader and her message become more intelligible if we let her personality and her work interpret each other. She makes, it is true, Terence Hewet say accusingly: »Nobody cares. All you read a novel for is to see what sort of person the writer is, and, if you know him, which of his friends he's put in. As for the novel itself, the whole conception, the way one's seen the thing, felt about it, made it stand, in relation to other things, not one in a million cares for that.»[5] But, in fact, as we have pointed out in an earlier chapter, she is constantly describing in her criticism »what sort of person the writer is»;[6] she hopes to get his vision right by relying in her interpretation on his background and personality. To be in quest for Virginia Woolf's personality as inter-related with her art is thus in keeping with her own method: it follows what she herself did in trying to find out »the way one's seen the thing, felt about it, made it stand in relation to other things.»[7]

By now we already know something of Virginia Woolf's inheritance. The stress has so far been on the intellectual advantages of being Leslie Stephen's daughter with hints of some emotional disadvantages, mainly resulting from the early death of her mother. At thirteen a child is beginning to pass through a phase when nothing in life is very easy. Both joys and sorrows become magnified and hard to bear. If to the general feeling of emotional unrest the major calamity of the mother's death brings additional disturbance, a shock, whose effects are in many cases far-reaching, is to be expected even in a normally sensitive child, much more in the super-sensitive

---

[5] *The Voyage Out*, p. 262
[6] cf. above p. 72, note 16
[7] vide above

Virginia Stephen. One is irresistibly tempted to dig for the roots of a later neurosis there.[8] The child's sense of security becomes shattered, which in itself alone may prove fatal. In addition, an imaginative and emotional child may become tied to the dead parent more tightly than she would have been had the parent been alive. We may not hold Freud's doctrines sancrosanct in everything, but his theory about the harmful effects of a child's reliance on, and too close relation with, the parents is proved to be true by innumerable examples taken from life. In Virginia Woolf's case, her constant preoccupation with death was partly caused by the frequent visits of death in her family during her most impressionable years, but it is not impossible that its almost morbid character had its origin in her excessive feeling towards her dead and idolized mother. The seeds of self-destruction were perhaps sown by her early unconscious or subconscious desire not to be separated from her, for with her also went the sense of security. Henceforth everything was constant change, motion, stormy wave-like movement. One is tempted to read into the role of waves, in her works as well as in her death, twofold symbolism, symptomatic of the character of her neurosis: they can be taken as a symbol of her sense of insecurity, of not being fixed anywhere, and as a recollection of the happy childhood days in St. Ives. In both cases their embrace meant a return to mother, to security.

But for Virginia Woolf — as for many others: take the Brontës, for instance, — art provided a beneficial outlet for locked-up emotions and actually proved her rescuer till new strains sapped her strength. In *To the Lighthouse* she returned to her childhood and tore open the unhealed wound in the same way she had returned to her nervous breakdown in *Mrs. Dalloway*, courageously, looking the monster bravely in the eye. Courage is, indeed, one of the most characteristic traits in Virginia Woolf. The will to face facts and to defy the lords

---

[8] Since writing this, what I heard from Leonard Woolf about Virginia Woolf's first mental breakdown after her mother's death confirms this conjecture.

of the unconscious by turning them into servants, as in *Mrs. Dalloway*, to write off the grim reality, may have helped her to prolong the struggle with weak nerves. Only those nearest to her knew how imminent the danger was all through her life, how hyper-sensitive she actually was. In *To the Lighthouse* we can measure the depth of the thirteen-year-old girl's sorrow by the success of Mrs. Ramsay's picture. Similarly by the success of the ironically affectionate picture of Mr. Ramsay we may measure the — perhaps unconscious — grudge she bore against her father, a trait well in keeping with the supposed mother complex, though not with the Freudian recipe. But, there was a strong element of masculinity in her; her theory of people being androgynous holds good in her own case. It is significant that one of the best-drawn figures in the book is little James[9] who, like Virginia Woolf herself, is in love with his mother and hates his interfering father. On the other hand, hate and love are near to each other. There may have been a mixture of both in her own feelings towards her parents. It would fit in well with her bisexuality which was perhaps too evenly balanced; the tension helped to create a state of neurosis. These are, however, only guesses in the attempt of an interpretation, and are bound to remain guesses till more material is available.

To the Lighthouse has generally been claimed by the critics to be Virginia Woolf's most satisfactory novel. One of the reasons of its success is said to have been the seclusion of the little group of intellectuals in their holiday resort.[10] Within that limited sphere — the critics say — everything can be made relevant to the pattern the author is weaving; she is freer to move in that particular area and the result is more satisfactory than if she had to exert fierce selection in her material by force, as it were. We can enlarge this somewhat and say that the secret of her success in *To the Lighthouse* lies at least partly in the fact that she is dealing with a familiar scene of her past life,

---

[9] James, Mr. Woolf tells me, was modelled mainly on Virginia Woolf's brother Adrian.

[10] cf. R. L. Chambers, op. cit. p. 40; D. Daiches, *The Novel and the Modern World*, p. 160, 184, E. Monroe, op. cit. p. 202.

with a period that had left the deepest marks in her soul. She is writing off something of her inner self. The details may or may not correspond to the actual fact, but the inner atmosphere is accurately true to reality. *To the Lighthouse* was written in 1927. In 1932 Virginia Woolf wrote for *The Times* an article on her father's centenary.[11] It is interesting to compare the two versions. The article states in sober prose what Virginia Woolf had more elaborately and fancifully worked out within the framework of Mr. Ramsay's picture. These is, naturally, no trace of the grudge which comes so clearly through in the book. Perhaps it had been got rid of for good and all — a salutary riddance, undoubtedly.[12]

In many respects Leslie Stephen, like Mr. Ramsay, must have been an exasperating father who excited »extremes of emotion in the breasts of his children, standing, as now, lean as a knife, narrow as a blade of one, grinning sarcastically, not only with the pleasure of disillusioning his son and casting ridicule upon his wife, who was ten thousand times better in every way than he was — —, but also with some secret conceit at his own accuracy of judgement. What he had said was true. He was incapable of untruth; never tampered with a fact; never altered a disagreeable word to suit the pleasure or convenience of any mortal being, least of all his own children, who, sprung from his loins, should be aware from childhood that life is difficult; facts uncompromising; and the passage to that fabled land where our brightest hopes are extinguished, our frail barks founder in darkness — —, one that needs, above all, courage, truth, and the power to endure.»[13] In that passage, one of the clues to Virginia Woolf's personality may be detected. It was a hard school where she learned not to take things at their face value. She gained wisdom and courage, it is true, but, even so, her loss may have been greater: at an early age she lost a child's natural sense of being protected. She was robbed of every illusion, and illusions, she says — from her

---

[11] included in *The Captain's Death-Bed and Other Essays*, pp. 67—73.
[12] cf. Annan on the subject, op. cit., p. 105 and 301
[13] *To the Lighthouse*, pp. 12—13

own bitter experience, undoubtedly — »are to the soul what atmosphere is to the earth. Roll up that tender air and the plant dies, the colour fades. The earth we walk on is a parched cinder. It is marl we tread and fiery cobbles scorch our feet.»[14] That is a poetic statement of what modern child-psychology holds for a fact. For a child, protective love is the foremost necessity in life. It has to have the illusion that its parents are capable of saving it from any calamity, that it need not fear. If it is robbed of those illusions by the act of the parents or by fate, the child's mental health tends to be undermined and later neuroses may be the result.[15] In *To the Lighthouse*, little James, with his complexes, is a poet's perhaps intuitive application of psychological theories, Freudian and other.

No one could, as a child, have better been aware than Virginia Woolf that life was hard and insecure, that death lurked at every corner. There was no heavenly father to turn to for help in her agonies, and the earthly father was not very reliable either; he was more in need of sympathy than any of the children could afford to be. If his little finger ached, the world was coming to an end. Like Mr. Ramsay's, his »immense self-pity, his demand for sympathy poured and spread itself in pools at her (Mrs. Ramsay's) feet, and all she did, miserable sinner that she was, was to draw her skirts a little closer round her ankles, lest she should get wet».[16] Significantly ever since her childhood Virginia Woolf disliked and distrusted the feeling of self-pity — in herself as well as in others. Leslie Stephen's was a splendid mind and his pursuit of truth admirable, no one is more willing to grant that than his daughter. But there was in it

---

[14] *Orlando*, p. 184

[15] This factor in the development of neuroses has lately been especially stressed, e.g., by Dr. J. A. Hadfield, in his *Psychology and Mental Health* (Allen & Unwin, 1950). While paying due attention to Freud and his theory of infantile sexual wishes, Dr. Hadfield has raised the feeling of deprivation of love, the repressed craving for love, to be one of the basic causes of psychoneuroses. Cf. also W. Stekel, *Lettres à une Mère* and *Education des Parents*, or Harald J. Schjelderup, *Nevrosene og den nevrotiske karakter*, Oslo.

[16] p. 236

something, as Virginia Woolf elsewhere says, »intemperate».[17] His tendency »to pursue truth with such astonishing lack of consideration for other people's feelings, to rend the thin veil of civilisation so wantonly, so brutally,»[18] was to her a horrible outrage to human decency. His fits of anger were sudden, violent, and unreasonable. Anything could happen at any time, even when they had guests. He might choose not to utter a word as when R. L. Stevenson and F. W. Maitland were once invited to dinner. Somehow Leslie Stephen, like Mr. Ramsay, seemed sometimes to have been made differently from other people, »born blind, deaf, and dumb, to the ordinary things, but to the extraordinary things with an eye like an eagle's».[19] When he stared at you with those steel-blue eyes of his, his look was so penetrating that it was as if he saw you »for ever», as his daughter puts it. Yet he was a human being that captured and held a fellow human being in bondage. He was so genuine, so childlike, so persevering and ardent in whatever he did. He was greatly enriched his daughter's conception of human personality, for, obviously, he was the early-conceived prototype of those complex human beings of whom she found it impossible to say that they were this or they were that. »How did one judge people, think of them? How did one add up this and that and conclude that it was liking one felt, or disliking? And to those words, what meaning attached, after all?»[20] One needs fifty pairs of eyes and a secret sense, »fine as air, with which to steal through keyholes»[21] to get that knowledge of another person which would entitle one to judge him, and, even so, one is inclined to distort what one sees, for one's private purposes. What knowledge, gained in childhood, can be more valuable for a future writer?

From the early years nothing was very simple for the daughter of a Leslie Stephen. No wonder she was a shy, gawky, highly-strung

---

[17] *The Common Reader* I, p. 278
[18] *To the Lighthouse*, p. 54
[19] ibid., p. 111
[20] ibid., p. 42
[21] ibid., p. 303

child. Later on her nerves gave way several times.[22] The second world war sapped her strength to the extent that she began to live under the growing fear of losing her mind again. Rather than go through that and perhaps never recover, she left a letter to her husband, walked towards the river Ouse near their house in the country and let the waves, which she had always so greatly loved, take her. Nervous breakdowns and insanity were, like early deaths, familiar in the family: Leslie Stephen's eldest daughter, who had inherited her weak nerves from her mother, had become mentally unbalanced at a fairly early age and never recovered. So had — as a result of an accident — his brother's talented son, the parodist J. K. Stephen.

In many ways life was grim for the sensitive child that Virginia must have been. But there were compensations. First of all the books in her father's library. Walter Pater's sister taught her Greek, but otherwise she got no regular education. She could follow her own tastes which led her to the best authors in English and continental literatures. Russian writers interested her greatly, at any rate at a later stage. From an early date the great authors of the world were automatically part of her rather haphazard upbringing.

Then there were young people for company, half-brothers and half-sisters, brothers and sisters, of whom Vanessa — Vanessa Bell, the painter — was Virginia's best friend. Painters and their art were always dear to her, perhaps, as we shall soon discuss in greater detail, because there was a great affinity in her own art to theirs: her imagination was mainly visual; she liked to paint, too, though in words. Lively young company was a healthy counterbalance to her natural tendency towards solitude. She learnt to love both talk and silence, to get mental satisfaction from action as well as inactivity. Life may have been grim for her, but it cannot have been dull.

The greatest delight in those days was, however, the yearly visit to St. Ives on the Cornish coast. One could stand many agonies strengthened by the thought of summers there. The waves of the

---

[22] vide above p. 106, n. 7

sea came to represent everything, death, beauty, terror, love, life. They became the embodiment of the unity she longed for and eventually found behind phenomena. In them dwelt security. When looking at them she felt »how life, from being made up of little separate incidents which one lived one by one, became curled and whole like a wave which bore one up with it and threw one down with it, there, with a dash on the beach«.[23] The beauty around her there almost choked her. She felt that she could »only offer a thimble to a torrent that could fill baths, lakes«.[24] It is interesting to follow in Virginia Woolf's books how the waves came to absorb an increasingly important place in the author's life and imagination. First having been a source of childish delight they turned into a medium of artistic inspiration, then gradually began to exert a morbid fascination, finally developing — to use a Freudian expression — into a symbol of the mother's womb, into which the human being longs to return. What happened on the Ouse on March 28, 1941, seems an almost natural outcome of a lifelong development.

The acute sense of beauty that Virginia possessed from her earliest childhood may have, after all, come more from her mother than from her father who gave her his integrity and uncompromising love of truth, as well as her intellectual equipment. Virginia was thinking of her mother in her description of Mrs. Ramsay who had in her veins »the blood of that very noble, if slightly mythical, Italian house, whose daughters, scattered about in English drawing-rooms in the nineteenth century, had lisped so charmingly, had stormed so wildly, and all her wit and her bearing and her temper came from them, and not from the sluggish English, or the cold Scotch — —«.[25] Only in reality the blood was French, not Italian — that of the Chevalier Antoine de l'Etang, one of Marie Antoinette's pages who had been with the Queen in prison till her death. His daughter married James Pattle of the Bengal Civil Service, a gentleman of

---

[23] ibid., p. 76
[24] *The Death of the Moth*, p. 12
[25] *To the Lighthouse*, p. 19

doubtful reputation and of riotous living, dubbed »the biggest liar in India». The Pattles had seven daughters, who were not only beautiful but also famous for their wit. French *esprit* and the imagination of a liar had made a good hereditary combination. The daughters became »scattered about in English drawing-rooms» by marrying Mr. Cameron, Mr. Mackenzie, Mr. Prinsep, Mr. Jackson who became Virginia's grandfather, Mr. Bayley, Lord Somers, and Earl Dalrymple. In London these beautiful, artistic and witty ladies soon founded their own realm, christened 'Pattledom' by a friend of theirs. Little Holland House was occupied by G. F. Watts, the painter, and in its Dower House Mrs. Prinsep gave parties where, as later in Bloomsbury, artists mixed with intellectual celebrities and fashionable hostesses. One of the most original in mind and remarkable for her sense of beauty was Mrs. Prinsep's sister, Julia Margaret Cameron, who had taken up photography as her hobby and was among the first to develop it into an art. There is an interesting affinity in her conception of art and that of her great niece.

Julia Margaret Pattle was born in Calcutta in 1815. In 1837 she married Charles Hay Cameron, fourth Member of the Council of Calcutta and successor of Lord Macaulay in that office. She was at the head of European society in India. But she was not only a great hostess and charming, impulsive, generous person, but also greatly interested in intellectual pursuits and in art. In fact, she showed some literary skill herself in her autobiographical fragment, called *Annals of my Glass House*. But her main interest lay in art. She had an extraordinarily keen sense of beauty, but not enough talent for recapturing it by means of painting. Yet her artistic nature was to find an outlet, though by the merest accident. When she was about fifty, her daughter presented her with a lens and a simple dark-box in order to give her something with which to while away her time, now that her children were grown up. She knew nothing whatever about photography and had to find out everything by trial and error. She had always greatly admired the soft contours of Italian masters, and her ambition now became to produce the same effect through photography. Through sheer ignorance she happened to take an out-of-focus photograph and noticed its possibilities in the creation of an artistic effect. In 1865 she sent some of her photos to an exhibition in Edinburgh, but her pictures and artistic methods met with criticism. Her ambition to recapture not only the features but also something of the inner man was not understood. Yet, even to-day, her portraits of Charles Darwin, Robert Browning, Alfred Tennyson, Henry Longfellow, Thomas Carlyle, G. F. Watts, Miss Thackeray, Mrs. Jackson and others, carry an unmistakable stamp. In some of them, like The Day Dream, and The Kiss of Peace, in which she presented beautiful young women, one can easily notice the influence of her Pre-Raphaelite friends, the Burne Joneses and Rossettis. What is especially interesting for us is that we can detect the same attempt at recapturing »the luminous halo», the »semi-transparent envelope surrounding us from the beginning of consciousness to the end»[26] that inspires Virginia Woolf to try to achieve a similar effect. Both were in pursuit of the idea behind the phenomenon, in the Platonic tradition.

We may here suitably leave the factual autobiographical details in *To the Lighthouse* and touch another layer of meaning in the book. An alter ego of the author is disguised in Lily Briscoe, the painter, in whose attempt to paint Mrs. Ramsay's picture first from the model and then, after her death from memory, we are allowed to follow something of the creative process in Virginia Woolf herself. She not only identifies herself with Lily Briscoe in her love of Mrs. Ramsay. but also through her presents something fundamental in her own art. Critics have been fond of likening her work to pictorial art. Cézanne, Matisse, Manet, Monet, Picasso have been mentioned in her connection; one critic[27] sees in her an expressionist, another an impressionist.[28] Her interest in painting is natural: were not her best friends, her sister Vanessa, Duncan Grant and Roger Fry, painters; endless

---

[26] *The Common Reader* I, p. 189
[27] Joseph Warren Beach, for instance, in op. cit. p. 485
[28] cf. Herbert J. Muller, op. cit. p. 40. Also see Eva Weidner, *Impressionismus und Expressionismus in den Romanen Virginia Woolfs*.

discussions on visual arts must have been her daily food.[29] But it is not by mere detached deliberation that she chooses to use colour-symbolism.[30] She really seems to think in terms of 'greens' and 'blues'. Her way of thinking is obviously associational, cumulative. The reader gets the impression that she creates in the same way as the painter proceeds with his colours, adding touches here and there. Her work seems to rely largely on the subconscious, to be a series of »little daily miracles, illuminations, matches struck in the dark».[31] Her task is made both easy and difficult by the wealth of the images which her mind keeps throwing up from its depths: »scenes, and names, and sayings, and memories, and ideas, like a fountain spurting over — —».[32] After a great deal of concentration and massing together of images, suddenly, in a moment of intensity, the right word, the right shape or colour, is hit upon, and in the act of creation a mystical awareness of the wholeness and unity that there is behind the phenomena becomes all-absorbing. »Quickly, as if she were recalled by something over there, she turned to her canvas. There it was— her picture. Yes, with all its greens and blues, its lines running up and across, its attempt at something. It would be hung in the attics, she thought; it would be destroyed. But what did that matter? she asked herself, taking up her brush again. She looked at the steps, they were empty; she looked at her canvas; it was blurred. With a sudden intensity, as if she saw it clear for a second, she drew a line there, in the centre. It was done; it was finished. Yes, she thought, laying down her brush in extreme fatigue, I have had my vision.»[33] Active though Virginia Woolf's subconscious and great her reliance on its working may have been, she was very strict in sifting the results and subjecting them to the judgment of her critical mind. Seeming formlessness became definite pattern. Her subconscious was not allowed to have the upper hand. On the contrary, her books

---

[29] cf. also her essay on Walter Sickert.
[30] as also pointed out by Daiches, *Virginia Woolf*, p. 85
[31] *To the Lighthouse*, p. 249
[32] ibid., pp. 246 ff.
[33] ibid., 319—20

usually took years to finish. Even essays and shorter articles were read and reread, written and re-written several times before publication.

Virginia Woolf's interest is all along being directed more towards the primary act of apprehending life than to life itself in all its aspects. In this she is again a mystic who waits for a 'vision'. Her approach to life is through exalted moments of revelation which for her are analogous with the moments of creation, with aesthetic experiences. It is an approach which inevitably tends to lose in breadth what it gains in depth. A poet's or a mystic's interpretation of life moves along from the particular to the general using short cuts, which for a novelist are not always possible without an omission of something fundamental from his particular method of expression. Virginia Woolf's weaknesses as a novelist are an illuminating example of that fact.

In her essay on E. M. Forster Virginia Woolf had spoken about »the paraphernalia of reality» which »have at certain moments to become the veil through which we see infinity».[34] The thing we are looking at, she says, is lit up, and its depth revealed. It does not cease to be itself by becoming something else. How to connect the actual thing with the meaning of the thing is the gist of her preoccupation. In the early novels »the paraphernalia of reality» is not always in a balance with the attempt to catch the meaning. So, for instance, still in *Jacob's Room* and *Mrs. Dalloway*. But in *To the Lighthouse*, and even more so in *The Waves*, Virginia Woolf manages to keep near enough to actuality, yet saturating it with what she calls 'her vision', i.e. the power of penetration into the mysterious core of things. There we experience a balanced intermingling of the two planes in the way we have it in, let us say, Cocteau's *Orphée*-film, or in T. S. Eliot's *Cocktail Party*, or in Kathleen Raine's *Travelling Fair*, to take some recent examples. Lily Briscoe is the author's mouthpiece again. She is in pursuit of reality other than the apparent phenomenon. It is almost an enemy, »this other thing, this truth,

---

[34] *The Death of the Moth*, pp. 108 ff.

this reality, which suddenly laid hands on her, emerged stark at the back of appearances and commanded her attention».[35] »This other thing» makes it imperative to reduce the group of mother and child that Lily is painting into »a purple shadow». Nowhere in her novels does Virginia Woolf better manage to combine realism with her Platonic idealism than in *To the Lighthouse* with its two planes of existence, that of »angular essences» and of »flamingo clouds».[36] Mrs. Ramsay is seen as she really is sitting with her son on her knee, concrete, true to life, and yet at the same time reduced to something eternal, »a purple shadow».

As to the third aspect, the presentation of values, the reader may be somewhat surprised to find out that the elements he expects, having been told how book-learned, sophisticated, arrogant, flippant, and clever Bloomsbury is, are simply not there in Mrs. Ramsay's life. She may have, like Mrs. Ambrose, her early variation, *Principia Ethica* for her bedside book, but she has hardly any time for reading and little energy left from her eight children and exacting husband. But she is in no need of book wisdom. Hers, like Mrs. Moore's and Mrs. Wilcox's in E. M. Forster's novels, is intuitive. »She knew with out having learnt. Her simplicity fathomed what clever people falsified. Her singleness of mind made her drop plumb like a stone, alight exact as a bird, gave her, naturally, this swoop and fall of the spirit upon truth which delighted, eased, sustained — falsely perhaps.»[37] Bloomsbury was over-clever. Everything was discussed into bits and pieces. The atmosphere was soaked with intellectuality, and mockery was the favourite pastime. But although Virginia Woolf was at times the first to conform to the tone, to analyse, to deride, to tear into pieces, *To the Lighthouse* shows that she felt the aridity of such an attitude and respected greater simplicity of feeling and thinking, that of her Victorian — and yet very un-Victorian — home. Mrs. Ramsay's story proves that Virginia Woolf was not only clever but

---

[35] *To the Lighthouse*, p. 245
[36] ibid., p. 21
[37] ibid., pp. 49 ff.

also wise, that her sense of values was as highly developed as her sense of beauty, that her heart was as capable of feeling as her intellect was of sharp analysis. She may have been in many ways a frightening person, a disillusioned and relentless critic of life and people, yet in her books she is shown to be a great lover of frail mortality. She may have been neurotic, but her message conveys a sane and balanced view of life. Her neurosis has — as the case with artists so often is — been turned in her books into mental health. *To the Lighthouse* is her great synthesis and therefore the most satisfying of her novels; it is her practical application of *Principia Ethica*, an object lesson in its creeds: states of mind are what matter, perfect human relationships, possible through love that is not self-seeking, the most hard-won achievements in life. Life, led as Mrs. Ramsay did, with a balance of mind and matter, can in itself be made a work of art, for it has the secret power of giving permanence to an evanescent moment. Like art, it resolves chaos into coherence. It »makes figures».

The Ramsays — Mr. Ramsay is a philosopher and university lecturer — have taken a summer cottage somewhere in the Hebrides where they return year after year with their eight children and an odd assortment of friends. There are with them Tansley, the atheist, Carmichael, who should have been a great philosopher but now spends his days in a benevolent lethargy caused by morphia; Bankes, the botanist; Lily Briscoe, the painter; and some young people, all of them in some way in need of protection. Mrs. Ramsay is a collector of lame ducks. Her maternal instinct is so strong that it envelopes everybody within reach. Luckily enough she has an object whose demand for sympathy and absorption of flattery is unquenchable. Mr. Ramsay has both an inferiority and a superiority complex and his soul is swung between the two. »It was sympathy he wanted, to be assured of his genius, first of all, and then to be taken within the circle of life, warmed and soothed, to have his senses restored to him, his barrenness made fertile — —.»[38] Fortunately Mrs. Ramsay has

---

[38] ibid., p. 62

made it her life's work to give back self-confidence to people. In her husband's case it is easy, for he is only too ready to believe her. Though knowing herself to be in some respects stronger than her husband, Mrs. Ramsay does not like to hear people say that he depends on her, to think that of the two she is the finer. For, luckily, she can reverence him as no one else in the world. Petty, selfish, spoilt though he is, a tyrant who wears his wife to death, till she feels exhausted, »a sponge sopped full of human emotions,»[39] yet he has a fiery unworldliness which knows nothing about trifles. All his weaknesses become unimportant compared with his gift »suddenly to shed all superfluities, to shrink and diminish so that he looked barer and felt sparer, even physically, yet lost none of his intensity of mind, and so to stand on his little ledge facing the dark of human ignorance, how we know nothing and the sea eats away the ground we stand on — that was his fate, his gift».[40] To be married to such a person is a great strain, yet the greatest human happiness.

Mrs. Ramsay herself has the valuable gift of penetrating through the layers of unessentials into the core of things. That is, her sense of values is highly developed. Her self-criticism and honesty are admirable. With her fifty years, sunken cheeks, and shabby clothes she is nothing to look at, she knows. But what she does not know is that her grey-eyed, Greek-nosed beauty still has the power of making even dried-up bachelors think of cyclamen and wild violets. »Wishing to dominate, wishing to interfere, making people do what she wished», are some of the accusations brought against her. She is prone to exaggeration as her husband admonishes her time and again; she is wilful, she is irrational. In her darker moments she even suspects that what she sometimes dares to put to her credit, is, after all, only vanity. »For her own satisfaction was it that she wished so instinctively to help, to give, that people might say of her, —O Mrs. Ramsay! dear Mrs. Ramsay, Mrs. Ramsay, of course!' and need her and send for her and admire her?»[41] She is constantly — but not morbidly, for

---

[39] ibid., p. 54
[40] ibid., p. 72
[41] ibid., pp. 68 ff.

she has a healthy sense of proportion also in self-criticism — made aware »of the pettiness of some part of her, and of human relations, how flawed they are, how despicable, how self-seeking, even at their best.»[42] Mrs. Ramsay does not like clever people, for in their eagerness to criticize they invent differences »when people, heaven knows, were different enough without that».[43] To some male reader Virginia Woolf may appear in *To the Lighthouse* to be on her warpath as a femininist, for her references to »female fecundity» as a contrast to »male barrenness» are frequent enough to draw attention. But though the author's sympathy is clearly on the side of Mrs. Ramsay, she is a great advocate of family life, within the sphere of which she sees human existence at its fullest. Even with its thousand little irritations it is the only complete life. But, as always with Virginia Woolf, love must leave some margin of freedom. Love, at its best, like solitude, the other necessity in life, becomes a source of mystic unity where one is immersed in peace, rest, eternity. The mystic in her is never far away. For her, at moments, the walls of partition between human beings can be penetrated by means of love, but only the kind of love that »never attempted to clutch its object, but, like the love which mathematicians bear their symbols, or poets their phrases, was meant to be spread over the world and become part of the human gain».[44] It is the greatest gift in life, for it means ability to restore order into chaos, »to choose out the elements of things and place them together and so, giving them a wholeness not theirs in life, make of some scene, or meeting of people (all now gone and separate), one of those globed compacted things over which thought lingers, and love plays».[45]

To the Lighthouse is divided into three parts. The first, *The Window*, nearly two hundred pages, only covers one day, within the framework of which a trip to the lighthouse next morning is being planned, the intricate relationships of the leading persons

---

[42] idem
[43] ibid., p. 19
[44] ibid., p. 77
[45] ibid., pp. 295 ff.

analyzed and each of them shaped into a clear-cut figure. The second, *Time Passes*, is one of the purest and the most beautiful pieces of word-painting in the English language. We learn of Mrs. Ramsay's death, yet she is, like Jacob Flanders, omnipresent in the love of the people who had been near her. The war had taken one of the sons, and the eldest daughter had, like the author's step-sister, Stella Duckworth, died only some months after her marriage. After ten years the cottage is being prepared to take in the rest of the family again. The third chapter, *To the Lighthouse*, describes how James, the youngest, who had always felt antagonism towards his father because he had been a disturbing element in the boy's relationship with his mother, at long last makes the trip, planned ten years earlier, to the lighthouse with his father. It is their last struggle; the fulfilment of the child's dream, then damped by the father, releases the tension, and the lighthouse becomes the symbol of unity that had cast its rays on Mrs. Ramsay's life. Her task is thus fulfilled.

X

Orlando

The narrowness and the 'drawing-room' atmosphere of Virginia Woolf's world have all along been easy targets for the attacks of the critics. One does, indeed, feel that the ultra-refinement of her characters with their constant cultivation of sensibilities has deprived them of something vital, of deep primitive emotions perhaps, and of the compelling urge towards action which is, after all, inherent not only in Mrs. Mop but in every human being. In the delicious banquet that Virginia Woolf has to offer, »the mere man» — says Prof. Muller[1] — »still yearns for a little red beef and port wine». One need not be a mere man to share Prof. Muller's yearnings. There are signs that Virginia Woolf, in her heart of hearts, hid the same desire. Perhaps one may venture the guess that at times she was feeling slightly tired of being a lady. She was too intelligent not to have felt that her in many ways sheltered[2] position narrowed her sphere of experience. The rough and tumble of ordinary life, in many ways a salutary and even necessary experience for an artist, passed her by like a thunderstorm of which she only heard the distant rumble. She cannot have helped realizing the handicap, for by nature Virginia Woolf was a realist. That aspect is best seen in her essays, where her love of everything virile, of the rough and joyous Elizabethans, for instance, or of the Greek ideal of a »well-sunned» human being, is so marked. Here we see the realist, the humourist,

---

[1] *Modern Fiction*, p. 326

[2] outwardly, materially sheltered; her struggle for life took place on the mental plane. As 'skinless' a person as her father, she suffered defeats and underwent agonies unknown to an ordinary man of action.

the potential lover of red beef and port wine who would much rather remain with the gentlemen at the table than retire with the ladies to their drawing-room gossip. But Virginia Woolf had her spiritual escapades. In 1928 she published *Orlando*, which is in various ways also a key to understanding its author both as a personality and as a writer. It is Virginia Woolf's step out of her ordinary sphere of experience: she is having a holiday from her complex and torturing self.

She is in a holiday mood, too, all worries left behind. She allows herself to be reckless, adventurous, even romantic. It is a St. Ives-spirit, produced by the blue skies above, the green waves lapping at one's feet, and the salty breezes tossing one's hair. It gives a sense of exhilaration and relief for her sake to witness her in this happy mood, with charming poise and bubbling spirits. Delightful whimsicality characterizes this book; its author's humour, always upon the alert, is at its best. There are virility and robustness about *Orlando* such as are not to be met with in the other novels.[3]

It is not incongruous that Virginia Woolf should thank her Bloomsbury friends for their help in the preface to *Orlando*, playful though its tone is, for the book is as much a Bloomsbury book as *The Voyage Out, Night and Day, Jacob's Room*, or *The Waves*. With all its elements of fantasy, it is a piece of writing by a highly cultured, sophisticated, intellectual aristocrat who takes culture and her own place in it so for granted that she need not feel self-conscious about it and can therefore treat it without any undue solemnity. It is just as much about civilization as Clive Bell's book. Virginia Woolf's wide learning and wordly wisdom as well as penetration into her own mind are needed for it. She can be admirably detached, amused and satirical in relation to her own self. Blackstone finds the self-mockery in *Orlando* to be a sign of an underlying defeat in the author and misses »the personal touch, the note of passion and pity which raised

---

[3] Joan Bennett in her *Virginia Woolf* does not count *Orlando* among the novels, but it is, surely, difficult to place it in any other category, as pointed out also by B. Ifor Evans, *Engl. Lit. Between the Wars*, p. 73

the novels to tragic heights».[4] Thoroughly acceptable as Dr. Blackstone's views on other points are, it is difficult to agree here unless 'defeat' is being used to mean something like 'permanent dissatisfaction'. Strict and exhausting self-criticism is indeed an important element in Virginia Woolf's mental make-up, and a leading characteristic in *Orlando*. As for personal touch, it can be found on every page of the book, both in style and in content. In *Orlando*, as Gruber[5] points out, Virginia Woolf gave vent to all the sentimental lyricism that she tried to repress in her other novels. Writing *Orlando* must have meant for her a feeling of expansion, an equivalent of daydreaming where she could cross the boundaries of time and sex.

Orlando does not, perhaps, reveal itself at the first reading in all its implications. It has, like T. S. Eliot's works, too many layers. It is interesting to notice that Virginia Woolf and T. S. Eliot have expressed their conception of the depth-effect of a work of art in very much the same terms. Both of them hold that to correspond to the different layers in the mind there must be different levels of existence also in the works of art. The greater a poem, a novel, a play, the more of these layers of consciousness are brought into action and the greater the artistic and emotional satisfaction that ensues. The first and crudest appeal is to the senses: the visual and rhytmic cravings of the reader become satisfied. Next, emotions and passions come into play, and, lastly, appeal is made to the ethical self, convictions and faiths are called upon. The appeal need not, even must not, be forced and aggressive. Suggestion and allusion are the artist's best weapons. Shakespeare is the best example of the manifold levels of appeal. T. S. Eliot's *Cocktail Party* could be taken as one of the most illuminating present-day examples.[6]

Orlando, at its surface level, is a biography, though a rather queer one, of Virginia Woolf's friend, Victoria Sackville-West, the

---

[4] op. cit. p. 132

[5] *Virginia Woolf*, pp. 21—22

[6] cf. Virginia Woolf: *The Moment*, p. 25; T. S. Eliot: *The Use of Poetry and The Use of Criticism*, p. 19; also I. A. Richards: *Principles of Lit. Crit.*, ch. 27, pp. 211—14

well-known author and member of a noble family who, like Orlando's ancestors, »came out of the northern mists wearing coronets on their heads».[7] Thomas Sackville, first earl of Dorset (d. 1608), was one of the favourite courtiers of Queen Elizabeth. He also collaborated with Thomas Norton in the writing of the first English tragedy, *The Tragedy of Gorboduc*, performed in 1561. The Sackvilles' family residence, the magnificent House of Knole in Kent, dating back to the fifteenth century, now donated to the State like so many other great houses, corresponds to Orlando's country house where we first meet him, a sixteen-year-old boy, practising at slicing a Moor's head in the attic. J. W. Cunliffe's theory[8] is that *Orlando* is really a fantastic celebration of Knole Castle with allusions to the adventures and achievements of its renowned inhabitants who have played such an important role in English political and cultural life. The surface story gives plenty of support to that theory. First of all, Virginia Woolf is very fond of the idea that something of people continues living in the places they have loved. Mrs. Dalloway fancies leaving part of herself to the streets of London, and to her old home, the rambling house in the country. In *Jacob's Room* the room, symbolically, is all that is left of the boy. Orlando, too, »who believed in no immortality could not help feeling that her soul would come and go forever with the reds of the panels and the greens of the sofa. — — The heart still beat, she thought, however faintly, however far withdrawn; the frail indomitable heart of the immense building.»[9] Orlando is said to have married a Spanish dancer, Rosina Pepita. In reality Pepita was Victoria Sackville-West's grandfather's mistress who bore him several children, among them Victoria Sackville-West's mother. The lawsuits that are mentioned in *Orlando* took place in reality and have been described in *Pepita*, Miss Sackville-West's biography of her grand-mother.[10] Orlando's poem, *The*

---

[7] *Orlando*, p. 16
[8] *English Literature in the 20th Century*, p. 250
[9] *Orlando*, p. 285
[10] published by The Hogarth Press 1937

Oak Tree, has its equivalent in V. Sackville-West's *The Land*, which, like Orlando's *Oak Tree*, won a prize in 1927. A poem quoted in *Orlando* is actually by V. Sackville-West. These matter-of-fact biographical details are, however, the least important elements. Several other themes can be detected in the book. Critics have various theories to offer. David Daiches[11] considers Orlando a symbolic figure, the main theme being the development of the hero-heroine through different phases to become finally the modern writer with a modern sensibility — a theory that no one can quarrel with. A. C. Ward[12] regards the book as, in part at least, a satire upon the contemporary fashion of writing books in which the Time convention is thrown to the winds — an explanation which contradicts Virginia Woolf's idea of the relativity of time which she expressly sets about to elucidate in *Orlando*. It is the discrepancy between the time of the outward happening and that inside one's mind that fascinates her. The self, »which has been blown about at so many street corners, which has battered like a moth at the flame of so many inaccessible lanterns,»[13] lives through many ages in the mind while its bodily counterpart may have a life, »shorter than a fall of a rose leaf to the ground».[14] — Virginia Woolf expresses in poetical terms what an Einstein or a Bergson have formulated in physics and philosophy. All three have come to the same conclusion, though through different channels of approach. — Delattre[15] draws attention to the name of the book. In his opinion the real subject is the problem of sexes: Virginia Woolf's Orlando is an amalgamation of Shakespeare's Orlando and Rosalind. And indeed, the atmosphere of the book is that of *As You Like It*, and Orlando's personality certainly an amalgamation. Joseph Warren Beach[16] gets ample support for his theory that *Orlando* is a study in multiple personality and a protest

---

[11] cf. *Virginia Woolf*, p. 93
[12] *The Nineteen-Twenties*, p. 63
[13] *The Death of the Moth*, p. 29
[14] *Orlando*, p. 92
[15] op. cit. p. 181, 189
[16] *The 20th Century Novel*, pp. 491—2

against the too narrow labelling of anybody. He considers Orlando an image for making vivid a philosophical abstraction, the truth of human nature. And a very complex truth Virginia Woolf always finds it to be. Let us take the seemingly simple and straightforward question of age, for instance. The author mentions Orlando's exact age, but considering that he lives through four centuries and yet has only reached thirty-five at the end of the book in 1928, man's age is obviously of no great importance. »Of some people», the author argues in defence of her point, »we can justly say that they live precisely the thirty-eight or seventy-two years allotted to them on the tombstone. The rest we know to be dead though they walk among us; some are not yet born though they go through the forms of life; others are hundreds of years old though they call themselves thirty-six. The true length of a person's life, whatever the *Dictionary of National Biography* may say, is always a matter of dispute.»[17] Orlando's life is an example of the development of a 'round' personality; he is the 'well-sunned' nature which Virginia Woolf admires in Plato: »the man who practises the art of living to the best advantage, so that nothing is stunted but some things are permanently more valuable than others».[18] The hero is, in short, an embodiment of the Bloomsbury ideals added with the spirit of famous English seafarers and adventurers. His life is full of intense emotional and intellectual excitement. His span of life is filled with rich experience and coloured with memories of ages-long family tradition, exactly as his creator's was. Only Virginia Woolf's family had used the pen for generations instead of the sword, and their sphere of experience had been confined to intellectual adventures.

The problem of the human mind, that »phantasmagoria» and »meeting-place of dissemblables»[19] becomes a matter of ever-increasing complexity in the light of the impact of a second on the mind and of the oddity of memory. »Time», Virginia Woolf reflects, »though

---

[17] *Orlando*, p. 274 ff.
[18] *The Common Reader* I, p. 52
[19] *Orlando*, p. 160

it makes animals and vegetables bloom and fade with amazing punctuality, has no such simple effect upon the body of man. The mind of man, moreover, works with equal strangeness upon the body of time. An hour, once it lodges in the queer element of the human spirit, may be stretched to fifty or a hundred times its clock length; on the other hand, an hour may be accurately represented on the time piece of the mind by one second.»[20] The so-called self becomes more and more confused. Clear-cut lines become impossible, and the task of the biographer precarious. To select the key-self among the thousands of selves that a person may possess, is no easy task. Personality is and remains an enigma and life a puzzle. To Orlando it seemed »of prodigious length. Yet even so it went like a flash. But even when it stretched longest and the moments swelled biggest and he seemed to wander alone in deserts of vast eternity, there was no time for the smoothing out and deciphering of those thickly scored parchments which thirty years among men and women had rolled tight in his heart and brain.»[21]

A human being having such hazy outlines and being so complex in content, the dangers of a biography as well as of autobiography are bound to be great, or, as Virginia Woolf puts it, »intimacy is a difficult art».[22] One must not be too sanguine about ever learning to know anybody well, not even oneself, least of all oneself. Perhaps because Virginia Woolf was so well aware of the dangers, she kept to the ordinary methods in her biography of Roger Fry; the result is nothing out of the ordinary either. In *Flush*, Elizabeth Barrett-Browning's biography, she presented a new angle of vision, that of the heroine's dog! This extraordinary angle does somewhat help to bring about the »luminous halo», even if seen through the innocent eyes of a lap-dog. Virginia Woolf was always anxious to experiment. In *Orlando*, she could be at her most reckless in trying to pierce the haze, as she was dealing with herself, trying to reveal »her own

---

[20] ibid., p. 91
[21] ibid., p. 93
[22] *The Common Reader* II, p. 201

secret springs of action and reserve»[23], which she set as an aim in autobiography. *Orlando* started partly as a family joke at the cost of the author herself and of her friend, of whom neither minded being the objects of an experiment. On the contrary, they must have enjoyed the adventure. *Orlando* ended by being a work of art, and an important link in Virginia Woolf's artistic development, with a great deal of self-revelation in it, and with passages of the most limpid beauty in English writing.

---

[23] ibid., p. 139

XI

A Room of One's Own and Three Guineas

Virginia Woolf's mind had been maturing mainly under the influence of her male friends and their Cambridge heritage. Her intellectual development had been stimulated early and disproportionately compared with her emotional self, which was perhaps a handicap in reaching a balance between the two. She was thirty when she married Leonard Woolf, one of her brothers' Cambridge friends, as intellectually sincere and uncompromising a human being as she was herself. The marriage turned out a success, a partnership where each enriched the other and acted as a stimulus. Obviously her husband understood and respected her urgent need of that independence and freedom which she so often stresses in her novels. »There is dignity in people», she says in *Mrs. Dalloway*, »a solitude; even between husband and wife a gulf; and that one must respect, — — for one would not part with it oneself, or take it, against his will, from one's husband, without losing one's independence, one's self-respect — something, after all, priceless».[1] Together the Woolfs established The Hogarth Press, which turned out to be a valuable instrument for spreading information on controversial and topical subjects as well as for bringing out books of great cultural and artistic merit. From its modest beginning in Richmond it grew into a publishing house of the greatest value in English life. Leonard Woolf's main interest lies in politics and sociology. His wife came to share his views. Together they toured the North Country industrial area taking part in political discussions. Both had left wing, Trade

---

[1] p. 132

Union sympathies, but they did not accept Marxism. On the contrary, Leonard Woolf calls »grotesque»[2] the assumption that the whole historical process, the ebb and flow of civilization should be determined by economic causes. If Virginia Woolf took part in her husband's political interests, Leonard Woolf, on his part, thoroughly agreed with his wife's activities in furthering the woman's movement. Several of the »suffragettes» were their personal friends, and although Virginia Woolf did not approve the violence of their methods, she gave her whole-hearted support to their cause.

She herself had no obvious personal grudge against men. She had »a room of her own and five hundred a year».[3] Thus no one could force her to do anything she did not want to do, and, happily, no one tried. There was no reason why she should not take men humourously, vanities and all, and have an amused laugh at the cost of an Oscar Browning who, in real earnest, declaimed that even the best woman at Girton or Newnham was intellectually the inferior of the worst man at men's colleges in Cambridge. But if there was a class of men that she did not take kindly to, it was the Oscar Brownings — perhaps the Leslie Stephens, too, for that matter — who »quote Aristotle at you over a friend herring and a pint of porter»,[4] or, like Mr. Hilbery, sit »editing reviews, or placing together documents by means of which it could be proved that Shelley had written 'of' instead of 'and', or that the inn in which Byron had slept was called the 'Nag's Head' and not the 'Turkish Knight', or that the Christian name of Keats's uncle had been John rather than Richard; for he knew more minute details about these poets than any man in England, probably, and was preparing an edition of Shelley which scrupulously observed the poet's system of punctuation».[5] How dried they were in her opinion, these clever men, how pitiable compared with a Mrs. Ramsay, how sterile and arid in their »prodigious learn-

---

[2] *Quack, Quack*, p. 23
[3] *A Room of One's Own*, p. 142
[4] *The Voyage Out*, p. 263
[5] *Night and Day*, pp. 108 ff.

ing and timidity», in their »wintry charm without cordiality», in their »innocence blent with snobbery»!⁶

A reason for that antagonism may be found in the fact that she may secretly have envied her male friends. Perhaps there was, after all, a sore point in her mind, a little more of personal resentment in her attitude than she would have cared to admit. Her brothers, like those of her friends, had been sent to Cambridge. She, like most educated men's daughters at that time, had to snatch what education she could in a haphazard way. For young intellectual women, Oxford and Cambridge were »like petticoats with holes in them, cold legs of mutton, and the boat train starting for abroad while the guard slams the door in their faces».⁷ She, for all her academic contacts, sometimes felt the lack of a sound university training and complained about it.⁸ And yet she was luckier than most, being almost overwhelmed with Cambridge influence indirectly. But she sometimes felt it a relief to get beyond its reach. Too much of it left her with a sense of being choked and made her feel occasionally rebellious. Second-hand influence can seldom help to make away with the sense of frustration that a lack of first-hand opportunity may create. So Virginia Woolf felt that she had to do what she could to guard women's intellectual freedom and to fight for their equality in having the same educational opportunities that men had as their birthright. Hence *A Room of One's Own* and *Three Guineas*. Men are too ready to come forward and say what a woman ought and what she ought not to do. Virginia Woolf cannot have that. She resents seeing »the bishops and the deans, the doctors and the professors, the patriarchs and the pedagogues all at her shouting warning and advice. You can't do this and you shan't do that!»⁹ She sternly refuses to turn off the grass at the call of the Beadle. »Lock up your

---

⁶ *Mrs. Dalloway*, p. 193
⁷ *Three Guineas*, p. 12
⁸ cf. *Letter to a Young Poet*, p. 7
⁹ *A Room of One's Own*, p. 141

libraries if you like; but there is no gate, no lock, no bolt that you can set upon the freedom of my mind.»[10]

Although rebellious, Virginia Woolf did not belong to those suffragettes who dressed in high collars and manly garments and stressed the similarities of the sexes. On the contrary, she was keenly aware of their differences and held that only by admitting those differences can both sexes develop their own qualities to the full without surrendering their special characteristics. Thus, when she draws plans for her women's ideal college in *Three Guineas*, she takes into consideration all the time that the future residents will be *women*.[11] *Three Guineas* is an aggressively femininist tract, not a work of art. Mrs. Leavis is not entirely wrong in her accusation of rash assumptions and exaggerations. But what Mrs. Woolf has to say about women's education and about the ideal college she plans for them, do not deserve derision. Here, as elsewhere, Virginia Woolf's aim is unity, combining a whole out of pieces. One side of life must not gain importance at the cost of the others. They are all important as parts of a whole: mind as well as body, thinking as well as living. We must be properly equipped for all. Co-operation is what is needed most in life — co-operation of mind and body, of different sexes, of human beings, of classes and races. Life means understanding, all-round integration. Thus, in her ideal women's college, Virginia Woolf abolishes competition, degrees, prizes, chapels, gowns, and other academic decorations. The curriculum is to include only those arts that can be taught cheaply and

---

[10] ibid., p. 114

[11] A heavy attack against *Three Guineas* and Mrs. Woolf was made by Q. D. Leavis in Scrutiny, Sept. 1938, pp. 203—14, under the title: *Caterpillars of the Commonwealth Unite*, cf. above p. 68. As an illustration of Mrs. Leavis's style a few sentences on the page 204 may be quoted: »*Three Guineas* is bad-tempered, peevishly sarcastic and incoherent — — — highly undesirable, a let-down for our sex. — — — not merely silly and ill-informed, though it is that too, it contains some dangerous assumptions, some preposterous claims and some nasty attitudes. — — — she tries to make a weapon of feminine inconsequence. — — — Mrs. Woolf's mental processes reminded him (a friend of Mrs. Leavis) of Mrs. Nickleby's.» And so on, for ten pages.

practised by poor people, for she cannot see that women can ever be rich. Medicine, mathematics, music, painting, and literature shough be taught, as well as the arts of human intercourse, »the art of understanding other people's lives and minds, and the little arts of talk, of dress, of cookery that are allied with them».[12] The recipes for a 'good life' remind the reader of Clive Bell's *Civilization*.

Though herself aggressive in *Three Guineas*, Virginia Woolf rightly held that aggressiveness is a sign of immaturity. Women, she says, are too self-conscious — »conscious of their own peculiarities as a sex; apt to suspect insolence, quick to avenge grievances — —».[13] There is no folly, she thinks, more distressing, either in man or woman, than being proud of one's sex. If only, she thought, women could get rid of their fear and bitterness, two of the greatest enemies of human freedom and, hence, of human happiness, their balance of vision would be restored. For her there is great dignity in womanhood, as shown by the pictures of Mrs. Ambrose and Mrs. Ramsay.

The importance of being of this sex or of that diminishes still more if we think, like Virginia Woolf, that, despite the profound differences, there is vacillation from one sex to the other, a curious intermingling of them, in the mind of every human being. This pet theory of hers is specially illustrated in *Orlando*, but reflections of it can be found in all her books. In *A Room of One's Own*, for instance, we find her wondering whether »there are two sexes in the mind corresponding to the two sexes in the body».[14] In the same way, she says, as the union of man and woman makes for the greatest satisfaction and happiness in life, in each of us two powers preside, one male, one female; in the man's brain the male predominates over the woman and in the woman's vice versa. The idea is not new, of course. In Plato we have the Androgyns; similarly the adjective 'androgynous' is used by Coleridge, for instance, of Shakespeare's mind to

---

[12] *Three Guineas*, p. 62
[13] *The Moment and Other Essays*, p. 96
[14] p. 147

express the highest creative power and the greatest freedom and lucidity of intellect. Virginia Woolf adds some other examples. Keats, Sterne, Cowper, Lamb, and Coleridge belong, in her opinion, to the androgynous.[15] Milton and Ben Jonson had a little too much of the male, whereas Proust has too much of the female. And, one might add, Virginia Woolf an equal amount of both.

Considering her theory of the duality of mind, it is only natural that she should ban femininist propaganda — although not the feminine point of view — from those of her books that aimed at high artistic standard — *Three Guineas* not being a work of art. According to her, a work of art is a result of a co-operation between all the elements of the mind. »Some collaboration», Virginia Woolf claims, »has to take place in the mind between the woman and the man before the art of creation can be accomplished. Some marriage of opposites has to be consummated. The whole of the mind must lie wide open if we are to get the sense that the writer is communicating his experience with perfect fullness. There must be freedom and there must be peace. Not a wheel must grate, not a light glimmer. The curtains must be close drawn. The writer, once his experience is over, must lie back and let his mind celebrate its nuptials in darkness. He must not look or question what is being done. Rather, he must pluck the petals from a rose or watch the swans float calmly down the river.»[16] *A Room of One's Own* contains some of Virginia Woolf's happiest descriptive passages and lyrical outbursts despite the fact that she was on her warpath there. She is thoroughly at ease in the book, and the reader is carried away by her felicitous similes and turns of phrase. Actually *A Room of One's Own*, in 1929, brought the author fairly far-reaching fame for the first time, for not only women, for whom she »had given a bible», as Swinnerton ironically puts it,[17] but everyone interested in good writing, enjoyed reading this feminine tract.

---

[15] cf. ibid., pp. 149 ff.
[16] ibid., p. 157
[17] op. cit., p. 279

It certainly is artistically fatal for a woman to speak aggressively as a woman, as Virginia Woolf repeatedly points out — *Three Guineas* being an illustration of the author's own fall into the trap — but a woman writer, she also insists, must not try to imitate a man either. »The weight, the pace, the stride of a man's mind are too unlike her own for her to lift anything substantial from him successfully.»[18] Take Jane Austen, for instance, Virginia Woolf's favourite English writer after Shakespeare; she never attempted to write like a man. Her achievement was the more remarkable as there was no tradition of really feminine writing so that Jane Austen can be called a pioneer. Her vision was of necessity still limited, owing to the circumstances of her secluded life. That excuse does not exist any more. Therefore the sphere of a modern woman writer need not and must not be more limited than a man's. She must be prepared, if the urge takes her, to write about all classes, all ages, all professions. But there is, in Virginia Woolf's opinion, one particular sphere where she must reign supreme as she has the easiest, even the only, access to it: her own soul »with its profundities and its shallows, and its vanities and its generosities».[19] A woman must tell »what your beauty means to you or your plainness, and what is your relation to the ever-changing and turning world of gloves and shoes and stuffs swaying up and down among the faint scents that come through chemist's bottles down arcades of dress material over a floor of pseudo-marble».[20] Sometimes the reader has an uneasy feeling that Virginia Woolf throws herself to unravelling the »profundities and shallows» with a perfect frenzy, almost tiring out herself — and the reader — in her quest. Nothing is too flimsy, too trivial, in that world of woman. One is at times inclined to agree with a critic who complains: »The gospel of the older writers centred round the commandment, 'Thou shalt select'. The pivot of the gospel declared by some modernists seems to be, 'Thou shalt not reject'.»[21] The lack

---

[18] *A Room of One's Own*, p. 114
[19] ibid., p. 135
[20] idem
[21] A. C. Ward *The Nineteen Twenties*, p. 53

of selectiveness in Virginia Woolf, as also R. L. Chambers[22] rightly points out, is of course due to the stream of consciousness technique — Proust and Joyce are many times more prolific. Virginia Woolf's argument is that everything has its place in the order of things and therefore also its value. In her style, too, a woman writer must reflect her own being. She must, above all, be natural, and try to recapture the floating images which rise up from the depths of her mind in their haphazard, incongruous way. To imitate the natural run of the voice in speaking, as Virginia Woolf did — master stylist that she was, capable of almost any acrobatics with her language — is not easy, for it has »a quality which none that has heard it can imitate — — for it is born of the air, and breaks like a wave on the furniture, and rolls and fades away, and is never to be captured, least of all by those who prick up their ears half a century later, and try».[23] That it was more difficult even for Virginia Woolf than we could have guessed from the seeming ease of her style, becomes obvious when we hear that she considered a good day's work done if, during the morning hours that she devoted to writing, she compiled four hundred words which she then re-wrote perhaps several times.

What are we to make of this extreme femininity of Virginia Woolf's? What side-light can it perhaps throw on her mental make-up? Its very excessiveness makes the reader suspect that it is something more fundamental than just an artistic device or a propagandist attitude. Not for a moment is the reader allowed to forget that the author is a woman. For all her warnings to others that it is fatal for a woman to be aggressive, there is more than a hint of an excess of femininity in her own writing. Subject matter, style, points of view, everything is consciously meant to convey a feminine effect. It is as if it were an obsession. Yet she had no reason personally to feel self-conscious as a woman. She was talented, respected in her circle of friends, had an understanding husband, her five hundred a year and a room of her own; she was not suppressed in any way.

---

[22] op. cit., p. 84
[23] *Orlando*, p. 192

She was luckier than most people. But perhaps that was just it. Elizabeth Bowen, who knew her personally, states for a fact that Virginia Woolf reproached herself for being privileged and sheltered.[24] — an interesting and illuminating piece of information. »From whence then», Elizabeth Bowen asks, »came this obsession of hers that women were being martyrized humanly, inhibited creatively, by the stupidities of a man-made world?»[25] She, on her part, thinks that the reason lay in the fact of Virginia Woolf's seeing the 'outside' world at one remove. Everyone knows indeed from experience how much greater imagined sorrows can be than the real state of affairs. But may there not be another explanation, the origin of which can again be traced back to her childhood? Virginia Woolf's femininism was undoubtedly a sign of social conscience, but there was perhaps also an element of self-pity in it, »at one remove», as it were, unconscious, for self-pity is a luxury of the weak. A courageous and proud woman like Virginia Woolf could not have afforded it, nor would she have liked to confess even to herself that there was an element of it in her feelings. Did she not find it one of the most unpleasant features in Mr. Ramsay?

It is thus a winding route along which we arrive at the motive of self-pity, leading again back to Mrs. Stephen's death. In her teens Virginia was suddenly deprived of the object of the most natural outlet of her affection. From now on she only had an idolized picture of her mother to worship and to weave dreams about — later on woven into the pictures of Mrs. Ambrose and Mrs. Ramsay. The capacity of feeling sympathy was a family trait. Was not Leslie Stephen used to lying awake during the South African war, thinking of the unknown soldiers in the far-off battlefields? Also Virginia's social conscience was easily roused. Her repressed mother-worship gradually came to embrace womanhood generally. Women became in her eyes martyrs, in need of protection, the lack of which she knew from her own experience. When she fought for women, she thus came

---

[24] op. cit., p. 82
[25] ibid., p. 81

to fight both for her mother and for herself as she was in her teens, left unprotected. The unconscious grudge she bore against her father for reasons already stated helped to heighten the severity of her attitude.

Her conjectural mother-love also seems to fit in with another trait in her: Virginia Woolf herself could be taken up as an example of her own theory, that of psychical hermaphroditism. She could herself be counted among the androgynous: she had the clarity of a man's vision; at the same time no one could have been more feminine in her way of thinking and in her reliance on intuition rather than logic. Ruth Gruber has in her illuminating study pointed out Virginia Woolf's interest in Lesbian tendencies which can be detected in Mrs. Dalloway's relations with Sally Seton or in Miss Kilman's attitude to Elizabeth for instance, or in *Orlando*. In many ways Orlando is a self-portrait and there is something of Clarissa Dalloway's attitude in Virginia Woolf. Like them, she may have experienced the sensation of »yielding to the charm of a woman. — — And whether it was pity, or their beauty, or that she was older, or some accident — like a faint scent, or a violin next door (so strange is the power of sounds at certain moments), she did undoubtedly then feel what men felt.»[26] There was a tug of war in Virginia Woolf: she wanted to be a man, but she also wanted to be a woman. This too even balance may have been part of her personal tragedy; it certainly contributed a decisive element to her artistic make-up. Perhaps it was because of her androgynous mind that she laid that extra stress on femininity? Perhaps she had to convince herself that she was either one thing or the other. And she chose to be stressedly a woman — at least in her art.

She managed to convince her readers anyway. If we follow the flow of criticism directed upon her, the epithet 'feminine' meets our eye constantly. But in the course of time it has in many studies on her become much less laudatory than it was for instance in Delattre's book, or Ruth Gruber's, Margaret Lawrence's or Gertrude Loh-

---

[26] *Mrs. Dalloway*, p. 36

müller's who all used Virginia Woolf's femininity as a searchlight illuminating her other qualities. Women critics, on the whole, find her feminine traits mainly attractive, even if not always an artistic merit. Not all women, though. Elizabeth Monroe, for instance, whose treatise is one of the most interesting of the shorter ones, is severely critical. She is especially irritated with Virginia Woolf's feminine aestheticism and lack of vitality, a complaint more common in the American criticism of Virginia Woolf than in that by the representatives of the older culture. Storm Jameson, it is true, who belongs to the latter group, accuses Virginia Woolf, for all her femininity with which she does not specially quarrel, of lacking humanity.[27] She thus joins the Americans, David Daiches,[28] William Troy, Conrad Aiken, Herbert J. Muller, to take some of the most important examples, who speak of Virginia Woolf's narrowness of approach to humanity. Their view of her is coloured by their social vision. Hence they generally find her Achilles heel to be mainly her detachment from the ordinary world.[29] Prof. Muller, no whole-hearted admirer of Virginia Woolf by any means, but a very fair critic, smells the old-fashioned odour of lavender when he approaches her works. For him, as for so many others, Virginia Woolf's feminity is too fragile to be a merit: she is for him hardly more than a Mrs. Gaskell in a modern dress.

That some of Virginia Woolf's characteristics, commonly termed feminine, irritate various readers, especially of the opposite sex, is actually no wonder. A greater wonder — and a triumph for her art — is that they irritate so few of them.

---

[27] *The Georgian Novel and Mr. Robinson*, p. 62
[28] emigrated to America from Scotland, now back at Cambridge.
[29] cf. above p. 97

XII

The Waves and After

By 1930 Virginia Woolf had established her fame and taken place in English literature as one of the most interesting authors and bold experimenters. She joined Dorothy Richardson and James Joyce as a writer who found her best method of expression in the stream-of-consciousness technique. It is quite likely that she would have chosen the inner monologue for her particular medium even if she had never read a word of either — or of Proust — in the same way as she embarked upon the Bergsonian idea of time before having read Bergson's works. The interest in silence already appears, as pointed out earlier, in *The Voyage Out;* from that the inner monologue is only a natural step forward.

In the thirties Virginia Woolf was at her most productive, though, perhaps, not at her best after *The Waves,* which appeared in 1931. *Flush* came out in 1933, *The Years* in 1937, *Three Guineas* in 1938, *Roger Fry* in 1940, and various shorter pamphlets and reviews in between them. *Between the Acts* was published posthumously in 1941, but it had been written in 1939. In 1932 she wrote *A Letter to a Young Poet* where she stated what she thought a poet's task was. Her definition is interesting in so far as every word of it can be applied to her own work, although she speaks expressly of poetry. A poet's task, she says, is »to find the relation between things that seem incompatible yet have mysterious affinity, to absorb every experience that comes your way fearlessly and to saturate it completely so that your poem is a whole, not a fragment; to re-think human life into poetry and so give us tragedy again or comedy by means of characters not spun out at length in the novelist's way, but condensed and synthesized in the poet's way — — —»[1] Hers was quite obviously the poet's way.[2]

Nowhere was she more a poet than in *The Waves*, the peak of her art.[3]

---

[1] p. 22

[2] Even if we agree with Elizabeth Bowen when she says (op. cit. p. 79) that there is no such thing as a typical Virginia Woolf-novel for she is constantly experimenting in something new, there is one thing that is overwhelmingly characteristic of her, and that is her interest in form. It is now fashionable to interpret artists in the light of neuro-pathology. In the latest book on Dickens (Julian Symons. *Charles Dickens*, London, 1951) for instance, he is shown — convincingly to my mind — to have been a victim of maniac-depression. Similarly Goethe's genius was tied to the 7-year cycles of mania and depression. Dostojevsky's masterpieces have long been considered as having been affected by his epilepsy. And so on. Virginia Woolf too is a tempting object in that respect. Genius cannot, of course, be explained away by any psychological theories, but its understanding is made easier through them. In Virginia Woolf's case resorting to Kretschmer is both interesting and rewarding. To a layman, at any rate, her work seems to prove what the psychologists have said about mind and matter being one, the physical structure and the quality of work being closely linked together. Virginia Woolf was a textbook example of a leptosome, and her neurosis was probably that of a schizophrenic. At any rate the characteristics of a schizo, as presented by Kretschmer (*Physique and Character*, pp. 150 ff., or *The Psychology of Men of Genius*, pp. 53 ff.) are easily applicable to her. She was a mixture of hypersensitiveness and coldness. Hers was the »light, intangible breath of aristocratic frigidity and distance, an autistic narrowing down of affective responses to a strictly limited circle of men and things», that Kretschmer speaks of (*Physique and Character*, p. 157). In schizos there is a tendency to constant self-analysis and an inner unrest from which they try to escape into some kind of mysticism. Virginia Woolf, when depressed, was filled with an acute sense of guilt. Her longing for unity resulted, as we have seen, in a kind of pantheism. Autism, i.e. living inside oneself, and a great capacity for splitting up one's conscious field into its elements are also components of Virginia Woolf's personality. Hence, perhaps, in her art she was untiringly concerned with the borderline between the conscious and subconscious areas in the human mind. Schizothyme artists, we are told, are primarily interested in form. What else is Virginia Woolf's art than constant reconnoitring in the no-man's-land that lies between prose and poetry, a constant quest for new possibilities in form?

[3] Critics have, by no means, been unanimous in their praise of *The Waves*,

Robert Peel,[4] to my mind very aptly sums up the real importance of *The Waves* as a work which achieved the complete statement of faith. »Her aesthetic faith appears here as what it has always really been, a religion. The form of the book is a sort of ritual; by means of it the author is able to break through appearances and limitations to the only reality that she acknowledges, the 'moment' as sensibility at its finest captures it. — — — Virginia Woolf's imagination is pantheistic, recognizing only love and death.»

The Waves is one more journey of exploration in search for goods which were by Bloomsbury considered ends in themselves: truth, aesthetic emotions and personal relations[5]. But truth, says the author, »is various; truth comes to us in different disguises; it is not with the intellect alone that we perceive it.»[6] Thus it is in solitude and in silence that truth is most likely to be glimpsed. Once more Virginia Woolf returns to her favourite theme: reality lies behind phenomena, not in them. The essence of human beings can only be captured by what they don't say. »— — — these attempts to say, 'I am this, I am that', which we make, coming together, like separated parts of one body and soul, are false. Something has been left out from fear, something has been altered, from vanity. We have tried to accentuate differences. From the desire to be separate we have laid stress upon our faults, and what is particular to us. But there is a chain whirling round, round, in a steel-blue circle beneath. — — — Yet these roaring waters — — upon which we build our crazy platforms are more stable than the wild, the weak, an inconsequent cries that we utter when, trying to speak,

---

though very few deny its beautiful and sensitive writing. What worries most of them is the word 'novel' in connection of the book. William Troy, op. cit. p. 350, calls its form »that of the extended or elaborated lyric». Peter Burra, in *The 19th Century and After*, Jan. 1934, pp. 112 ff., would not like to apply the word 'novelist' to VW at all; Rose Macaulay, *The Spectator*, 11. 4. 41. Vol. 5885, p. 394 ff., calls her a poet »writing a poet's prose from a poet's angle».

[4] in *The Criterion*, Oct. 1933, Vol. XIII, No. L, pp. 78 ff.
[5] cf. *The Moment and Other Essays*, p. 110
[6] *The Common Reader* I, pp. 41—42

we rise; when we reason and jerk out these false sayings, — 'I am this; I am that'. Speech is false.»[7] In *The Waves* Virginia Woolf's ambitious aim is to show the six characters at their barest, when all the superficialities, fears and vanities have been shed. We are therefore led into their personalities through an unusual door, a backstage door, as it were, to see the actors in their dressing-rooms without any make-up on. Nothing but the continuous monologues one carries on in one's mind is recorded. Yet we get a clear picture of the growth of the six personalities from childhood into their old age. It is a feat of unusual dimensions for a novelist!

The Waves is to a very great extent a Bloomsbury book. The six main characters remind us of the sophisticated, analytical, reasoned minds of the group of friends. Even Percival, the representative of anti-intellectualism, is anti-intellectual, sensuous, pagan, magnificent, simple, earth-bound in a way Bloomsbury specially valued. »Being naturally truthful, he did not see the point of these exaggerations, and was borne on by a natural sense of the fitting. was indeed a great master of the art of living so that he seems to have lived long, and to have spread calm round him, indifference one might almost say, certainly to his own advancement, save that he had also great compassion.»[8] Stephen Wonham in E. M. Forster's *Longest Journey* is the same kind of contrast to Rickie as Percival is to his friends, and idolized for the same reasons. They represent the Greek element, an intellectual's admiration of physical beauty and prowess, the radiance of primitive life.[9]

In the same way as Clarissa Dalloway, the nonentity, was made a mouthpiece of a transcendental theory, Percival, through his death, becomes the central figure in *The Waves*. Death is the »off-stage evil» that Angus Wilson speaks of in his talk on Virginia Woolf[10]

---

[7] *The Waves*, pp. 98—99

[8] ibid., p. 111

[9] Interesting side-light is thrown by Kretschmer, *The Psychology of Men of Genius*, p. 27, on the cult of friendship and the admiration of Greek sculpture which often go hand in hand.

[10] *The Listener*, Aug. 24, 1950, Vol. XLIV, No. 1126, pp. 279 ff.

rather than the pressing problem of evil, which he thinks to be symbolized through »the stamping beast», which is a recurrent image in the book. In Wilson's opinion the problem of evil is inadequately solved by Virginia Woolf and that is what is responsible for the unsatisfactory structure of her novels. But Virginia Woolf never even tried to solve the problem of evil; she left the appalling quality of the world at that. Who, for that matter, has solved the problem? Surely no one adequately. In *The Waves* as in her other works, Virginia Woolf accepts the cruelty of nature, the instability of life, »that emerging monster to which we are attached».[11] Any permanence that there may be in our »sleeping, eating, breathing, so animal, spiritual lives»[12] is invested in what is symbolic — that is the leading theme in Virginia Woolf's books, the joining thread in the skein of ideas. The sense of transitoriness was always with her, and her longing for permanence led her, as we have seen, along the mystic's path towards pantheism. In *The Waves* it is stressed by the individual lives being installed — by eight prose-poems that precede the eight parts of the book — against their cosmic background. The span of human life is shown adjusted to the march of day across the sky. The sun moves majestically in its orbit; the waves ebb and flow rhythmically while the world is wandering through abysses of infinite space. »It roars; the lighted strip of history is past and our Kings and Queens; we are gone; our civilisation; the Nile; and all life. Our separate drops are dissolved; we are extinct, lost in the abysses of the time, in the darkness.»[13]

Nowhere in her novels does Virginia Woolf so painfully feel the inadequacy of words as a medium of conveying the symbolic content of a familiar experience. Although *The Waves* illustrates the common experience, it is not linked to every-day life by the same use of seeming trivialities as in the earlier novels. It takes a further step in a contrary direction, towards the depths of the mind, into the

---

[11] *The Waves*, p. 47
[12] ibid., p. 176
[13] ibid., p. 160

borderline of the irrational and the subconscious, into a region where the accepted common language is not enough — of which *Ulysses* and *Finnegan's Wake* offer the best examples. Virginia Woolf, too, feels the need of »some little language such as lovers use, broken words, inarticulate words like the shuffling of feet on the pavement.»[14] The adjectives she uses tumble suggestively on top of each other: »a painful, guttural, visceral, also soaring, lark-like, pealing song»[15] bores itself into the reader's mind, although the author herself finds words inadequate and is dissatisfied with »these flagging, foolish transcripts, how much too liberate, how much too reasonable!»[16] Music, and »the silent kingdom of paint»,[17] would offer much better adaptable ways of expression than words.[18] She tries — without discarding the normal language — to come as near to both in her language as possible, especially in *The Waves*, where the rhythm and the word-painting form an essential part of its attraction.

In the 'thirties' Virginia Woolf was brought in close contact with the woman's cause. *A Room of One's Own* had come out in 1929. In 1931 she was asked to write an introduction to a collection of biographical sketches by well-known suffragettes, called *Life As We Have Known It*, and she attended their meetings to get material for her introduction. The introduction was not the only result: *The Years* and *Three Guineas* were to be further by-products.

The Years is Mrs. Woolf's counterblast to Galsworthy's *Forsyte Saga*. She had blamed him for being a materialist in his way of treating the theme. Now she herself attempted to write a novel proper which was yet to differ from *The Forsyte Saga* as completely

---

[14] ibid., p. 169

[15] ibid., p. 177

[16] idem

[17] *Essay* on *Walter Sickert*, p. 13

[18] »I always think of my books as music before I write them,» she says (vide quotation in R. C. Trevelyan's article in *The Abinger Chronicle*, Vol. 2, No. 3, pp. 23—4.) I. Verga has particularly drawn attention to Virginia Woolf's point-counter-point pattern. She compares her specially with Debussy, cf. op. cit., p. 5

as possible. *The Years*, indeed, is also a family chronicle, but that is its only similarity to Galsworthy's book. The span of Mrs. Woolf's novel, describing the life of the Pargiter family, covers some fifty odd years till the present time, i. e. 1937, the time of the writing. It is a bleak picture of a middle-class milieu, stripped of every make-believe garment, of all the superfluities that might create an illusion of 'niceness'. The Pargiter landscape is a barren country. In the foreground a half-rotten tree overshadows the growths underneath and around, so that they are withered and yellow from lack of sun. Colonel Abel Pargiter, a retired officer, is an insignificant human being, a Philistine, and a tyrant conforming to the custom of the Victorian age. Everything about the Pargiters is sordid when the scene opens; the mother is expected to die any moment, but drags on and on, so that even death, when it comes at last, has lost its dignity. Colonel Pargiter has a sordid mistress tucked away in a squalid back street. For the first time Virginia Woolf thinks it worth while describing someone whose emotions have become dried up, till only lust is left.

The Partiger family is fairly well off. The sons are well educated and become dons and barristers and other useful members of society. It is in the daughters' lives that bleakness dwells. The theme of *A Room of One's Own* and of *Three Guineas* is woven into the novel. The Pargiter girls are in the position of the ordinary Victorian middle-class daughters: unless they marry, there is not much they can do except private charity work, or else they have to enter the camp of the rebels. Eleanor, the eldest of the Pargiter daughters remains with Papa. She is »a well-known type, with a bag; philanthropic; well nourished; a spinster; a virgin; like all the women of her class, cold, her passions have never been touched; yet not unattractive.»[19] She is not by nature one of the rebels, like her sisters, the firebrands of the family, who take up 'the cause'. Eleanor's life drags on with Papa, until, middle-aged, she becomes free for the first time in her life to do what she likes. She makes the most of her freedom by

---

[19] *The Years*, p. 108

travelling and widening her mind. Imprisonment with Papa has not been able to quench her natural curiosity. Every moment is a miracle and a wonder. Eleanor remains the untiring questioner, the *alter ego* of the author, returning to the old theme again and again: »Is there a pattern in life», she keeps on wondering, »a theme, recurring like music; half remembered, half foreseen, — — — a gigantic pattern, momentarily perceptible?»[20] But there is still no answer. It seems as if there were, that is all that can be said. The present moment is all that matters. »She felt that she wanted to enclose the present moment; to make it stay; to fill it fuller and fuller, with the past, the present and the future, until it shone, whole, bright, deep with understanding.»[21] It is significant of Virginia Woolf's brand of femininism that it is Eleanor who is the nearest approach to a complete human being in *The Years* and not, for instance, Peggy, Eleanor's niece, a young psychiatrist, who had had all the advantages in life that her fighting aunts have with their sacrifices been able to secure for the younger generation. Virginia Woolf does not want to overestimate the influence of material advantages, important though they are in human development. She does not allow her anger to lead her astray in the estimation of human values.

The half-century through which we intermittently follow a family's life in *The Years* show the author in a different light from that of her previous novels. It is now the angry Virginia Woolf of *Three Guineas*, embittered by the injustices of society. Formerly she had concentrated on human beings as solitaries, or in their relations to other individual human beings, each dwelling in his or her ivory tower. Now she brought her figures down to the earth and found the contact exasperating. So far she had moved in the highly intellectual and disciplined world of her own set, where integrity and 'sweet reasonableness' were taken for granted as hallmarks, flawed and incomplete though the individuals in many other respects may have been. For the first time Virginia Woolf

---

[20] ibid., p. 398
[21] ibid., p. 462

stepped into the Philistine world and found her sojourn there an agony. It grieved her to admit that the Colonel Pargiters are the common representatives of the human species and the unworldly, even if egotistic, Mr. Ramsays the uncommon ones. *The Years* is as 'debunking' in its treatment of society as Lytton Strachey's biographies are of individuals.

In her last novel Virginia Woolf appears calmer and more optimistic again. She returns to her favourite theme: it is 'between the acts' that the significant dramas in human life are acted, it is in silence that the greatest emotions are expressed. Between the acts of a pageant, performed on a June afternoon in 1939 by the village people on the premises of Pointz Hall, the country house of the Oliver family, a worldless drama is acted by Giles Oliver and his wife, Isa. Love, hate and peace are the ingredients of their personal performance; those three are the elements that make the ply of human life: thesis and antithesis leading to synthesis.

While Giles and Isa are involved in their individual drama between the acts, the pageant proceeds, forming a large-scale background to a seemingly small-scale human intricacies. It reminds the reader of *Orlando* insofar as the scenes are a survey of English history, different episodes being illustrated through characteristic features of the respective periods. England in prehistoric times begins the pageantry. Chaucer's England is illustrated by Canterbury pilgrims, the Elizabethan age, Queen Anne's reign, and Victorian England are floodlit by means of plays within the play, and, lastly, »the present time. Ourselves», is described by help of cacophonous music suggesting the disintegration of society, the ruin of civilization. »Ourselves» are caught by flashes of bright surfaces of tin cans, candlesticks, and mirrors which the actors and actresses hold in front of the surprised audience, leaping and dancing around them, catching a nose here, a skirt there, glimpses only of the whole. »Scraps, orts and fragments, are we, also, that?»[22] the audience is left wondering, not quite able to make out what is meant by it all. The vicar of the village, in his

---

[22] *Between the Acts*, p. 221

speech of thanks, ventures an explanation: to him the play conveyed the idea that we are all part of the whole, of »a spirit that inspires, pervades . . . (The swallows were sweeping round him. They seemed cognizant of his meaning. Then they swept out of sight.)»[23] Human mind and nature, immersed in one unity; everything a part of a whole: yet another illustration of a pantheist's substitute for a personal salvation. »Somewhere, this cloud, this crust, this doubt, this dust — she waited for a rhyme, it failed her; but somewhere surely one sun would shine and all, without doubt, would be clear.»[24]

Between the Acts was published posthumously and, despite its fragmentariness, makes a summary of a lifetime's quest of beauty and truth. In *The Waves* Virginia Woolf makes Bernard say: »Some people go to priests; others to poetry; I to my own heart, I to seek among phrases and fragments something unbroken —.»[25] Virginia Woolf's friends in Cambridge had, in their attempts to get at truth, been charmed by G. E. Moore's method of reducing the reference of words to its minimum: »Do we desire to desire to desire to desire» was their verbal method towards revelation. Virginia Woolf discarded their scientific use of words and moved in the other direction; she tried to enlarge the meaning: hers was the emotive use.[26] For her, words have a twofold content, the evocative and symbolic as well as the direct and familiar. The twofold use of words corresponded, as it were, to the two dominating features in her nature. On one hand she was a rationalist and a realist, on the other, a mystic who accepted Blake's definition of reason as being »an inferior kind of knowledge». The former may be referred to her inheritance and environment, the latter may be said to be the emanation of her particular genius, of her true self, the combination of her body and soul, artistic to the core. Both qualities are essential factors in her. Through a touch of

---

[23] ibid., p. 224
[24] ibid., p. 76
[25] *The Waves*, p. 189
[26] cf. I. A. Richards, *Principles of Lit. Crit.* p. 267, on the definition of the two uses of language.

mysticism, reality in her art, in its deliberately limited sphere of experience, is made truly real, the erratic, the undependable made permanent. That, surely, is the hallmark of all true art, and makes for permanence in hers, also.

Bibliography

A. *Virginia Woolf's Works.*
(Publisher The Hogarth Press, London, unless differently stated.)

1. Novels.
    The Voyage Out. 1915. 458 pp.
    Night and Day. Duckworth & Co. London 1938 (1919). 538 pp.
    Jacob's Room. 1947 (1922) 176 pp.
    Mrs. Dalloway. Chatto & Windus London 1947 (1925). 213 pp.
    To the Lighthouse. 1946 (1927). 320 pp.
    Orlando. A Biography. 1949 (1928). 299 pp.
    The Waves. 1950 (**1931**). 211 pp.
    The Years. 1937. 469 pp.
    Between the Acts. 1941. 256 pp.

2. Short Stories and Sketches.
    Two Stories (in Collaboration with Leonard Woolf) 1917.
    The Mark on the Wall. 1919 (1917). 10 pp.
    Kew Gardens. 1919. 14 pp.
    Monday or Tuesday. 1921. 91 pp.
    A Haunted House and Other Short Stories. 1947 (1944). 124 pp.

3. Essays and Critical Writings.
    Mr. Bennett and Mrs. Brown. 1924. 24 pp.
    The Common Reader. First Series. 1948 (1925). 305 pp.
    Victorian Photographs of Famous Men and Fair Women, by I. M. Cameron. With Introductions by Virginia Woolf and Roger Fry. 1926. 15 pp.
    A Sentimental Journey through France and Italy, by Laurence Sterne. With an introduction by Virginia Woolf. Oxford University Press 1948 (1928) XVII. 233 pp.
    A Room of One's Own. 1946 (1929). 172 pp.
    On Being Ill. 1930. 34 pp.
    Beau Brummel. New York 1930. 12 pp.
    Street Haunting. 1930. 10 pp.
    Life As We Have Known It, by Co-operative Women. Edited by Margaret

Llewelyn Davies. With an Introductory Letter by Virginia Woolf. 1931 (1931) XXXIX. 141 pp.
The Common Reader. Second Series. 1948 (1932). 270 pp.
A Letter to a Young Poet. Hogarth Letters No. 8. 1932. 28 pp.
Walter Sickert. A Conversation. 1934. 28 pp.
Three Guineas. 1947 (1938). 329 pp.
The Death of the Moth and Other Essays. 1947 (1942). 157 pp.
The Moment and Other Essays. 1947. 191 pp.
The Captain's Death-Bed and Other Essays. 1950. 224 pp.

4. Biographies.
Flush. 1947 (1933). 163 pp.
Roger Fry. 1940. 301 pp.
Reviewing. With a Note by Leonard Woolf (Hogarth Sixpenny Pamphlets No. 4) 1939. 31 pp.

B. *Reference Books*.

ANNAN, NOEL GILROY, *Leslie Stephen*. His Thought and Character in Relation to his Time. Mac Gibbon & Kee. London 1951. 342 pp.

ARNOLD, MATTHEW, *Essays in Criticism* I—II. London 1905. XVI. 288 pp.

BEACH, JOSEPH WARREN, *The Twentieth Century Novel*. Studies in Technique. The Century Co. New York — London 1932. VIII. 569 pp.

BELL, CLIVE, *Civilization*. An Essay. Penguin Books. 1947 (1928). 157 pp.

BENNETT, JOAN, *Virginia Woolf*. Her Art as a Novelist. Cambridge University Press 1945. 131 pp.

BLACKSTONE, BERNARD, *Virginia Woolf*. A Commentary. The Hogarth Press London 1949. 256 pp.

BOWEN, ELIZABETH, *Collected Impressions*. Longmans Green & Co. London 1950. 245 pp.

CAMERON, JULIA MARGARET, *Victorian Photographs of Famous Men and Fair Women*. With Introductions by Virginia Woolf and Roger Fry. The Hogarth Press London 1926. 15 pp.

CECIL, LORD DAVID, *Poets and Story-Tellers*. A Book of Critical Essays. Constable London 1949. 201 pp.

CHAMBERS, R. L., *The Novels of Virginia Woolf*. Oliver and Boyd Edinburgh London 1947. 102 pp.

CONNOLLY, CYRIL, *Enemies of Promise*. Routledge & Sons Ltd. London 1938. VIII. 340 pp.

CUNLIFFE, J. W., *English Literature in the 20th Century*. The Macmillan Co. New York 1933. 341 pp.

DAICHES, DAVID, *Virginia Woolf*. PL. Editions Poetry London 1945. 151 pp.

Daiches, David, *The Novel and the Modern World*. The University of Chicago Press Chicago 1938. X. 224 pp.

Delattre, Floris, *Le roman psychologique de Virginia Woolf*. Librairie Philosophique. J. Vrin Paris 1932. 268 pp.

Dickinson, Goldsworthy Lowes, *After Two Thousand Years*. A Dialogue Between Plato and a Modern Young Man. Allen & Unwin London 1930. 213 pp.

—»— *The Magic Flute*. A Fantasia. Allen & Unwin London 1920. 127 pp.

—»— *J. Mc. T. E. McTaggart* with chapters by Basil Williams & S. V. Keeling (with portraits). Cambridge University Press 1931. VIII. 160 pp.

Drew, Elizabeth A., *The Modern Novel*. Some Aspects of Contemporary Fiction. Jonathan Cape Ltd. London 1926. VIII. 274 pp.

Eliot, T. S., *The Use of Poetry and the Use of Criticism*. Studies in the Relation of Criticism to Poetry in England. Faber & Faber 1948 (1933). 156 pp.

—»— *Notes Towards the Definition of Culture*. Faber & Faber London 1948. 124 pp.

Emerson, P. H., *Mrs. Cameron* with a descriptive Essay. Kegan Paul, Trench, Trübner & Co. London 1890 (Sun Artists No. 5, Oct. 1890). 10 pp. + 4 enlarged photographs.

Evans, B. Ifor, *English Literature between the Wars*. Methuen & Co. London 1948. 133 pp.

Forster, E. M., *Goldsworthy Lowes Dickinson*. Edward Arnold & Co. 1947 (1934). 277 pp.

—»— *Virginia Woolf*. The Rede Lecture 1941. Cambridge University Press 1942. 27 pp.

—»— *What I Believe*. The Hogarth Press London 1939. 22 pp.

Fry, Roger, *The Artist and Psycho-Analysis*. The Hogarth Press London 1924. 19 pp.

Gruber, Ruth, *Virginia Woolf*. A Study. Verlag von Bernhard Tauchnitz Leipzig 1935. 100 pp. (Kölner Anglistische Arbeiten 24. Band.)

Hadfield, J. A., *Psychology and Mental Health*. Allen & Unwin London 1950. 444 pp.

Harrod, R. F., *The Life of John Maynard Keynes*. Macmillan & Co. Ltd. London 1951. XIV. 674 pp.

Hoare, Dorothy, *Some Studies in the Modern Novel*. Chatto & Windus London 1938. 154 pp.

Holtby, Winifred, *Virginia Woolf*. Wishart & Co. London 1932. 205 pp.

Jameson, Storm, *The Georgian Novel and Mr. Robinson*. William Heinemann London 1929. 75 pp.

—»— *The Writer's Situation* and Other Essays. Macmillan & Co. Ltd. 1950. 200 pp.

JOHNSON, R. BRIMLEY, *Some Contemporary Novelists* (Women). Leonard Parsons London 1920. 220 pp.

KEYNES, JOHN MAYNARD, *Two Memoirs*. Dr. Melchior: A Defeated Enemy and My Early Beliefs. Introduced by David Garnett. Rupert Hart-Davies London 1949. 106 pp.

KRETSCHMER, ERNST, *The Psychology of Men of Genius*. Kegan Paul & Co. London 1931. XX. 256 pp.

—»— *Physique and Character*. Kegan Paul & Co., London 1936 (1925) XVI. 278 pp.

LAWRENCE, MARGARET, *The School of Femininity*. A Book For and About Women As They Are Interpreted Through Feminine Writers of Yesterday and Today. Frederick A. Stokes Co. New York 1936 XII. 382 pp. (published in London 1937 under the name of *We Write as Women*. Michael Joseph Ltd. 314 pp.).

LEAVIS, F. R., *The Common Pursuit*. Chatto & Windus London 1952. 307 pp.

LOHMÜLLER, GERTRUDE, *Die Frau im Werk von Virginia Woolf*. Ein Beitrag zur psychologischen und stilistischen Untersuchung des neuesten englischen Frauenromans. Universitätsverlag von Robert Noske in Leipzig 1937. (Aus Schrifttum u. Sprache der Angelsachsen. Band 8.) 102 pp.

LUCAS, F. L., *Literature and Psychology*. Cassell & Co. London 1951. 340 pp.

MACCARTHY, DESMOND, *Criticism*. Putnam London & New York 1932. XII. 311 pp.

—»— *Leslie Stephen*. The Leslie Stephen Lecture Delivered before the University of Cambridge on 27 May 1937. Cambridge University Press 1937. 46 pp.

MAITLAND, FREDERIC WILLIAM, *The Life and Letters of Leslie Stephen*. Duckworth & Co. London 1906. VIII. 510 pp.

MEREDITH, GEORGE, *The Egoist*. A Comedy in Narrative. Revised Edition. Staples Press London — New York 1948 (1879). VI. 393 pp.

MONROE, N. ELIZABETH, *The Novel and Society*. A Critical Study of the Modern Novel. The University of North Carolina Press Chapel Hill 1941. VI. 282 pp.

MOORE, GEORGE EDWARD, *Autobiography* vide Schilpp, P. A. (ed.). *The Philosophy of G. E. Moore*. (The Library of Living Philosophers, vol. 4.)

—»— *Principia Ethica*. Cambridge University Press 1903. XXVII. 232 pp.

MUIR, EDWIN, *Transition*. Essays on Contemporary Literature. The Hogarth Press London 1926. IX. 218 pp.

MULLER, HERBERT J., *Modern Fiction*. A Study of Values. Funk & Wagnalls Co. New York and London 1937. XVI. 447 pp.

Myers, L. H., *The Root and the Flower*. Jonathan Cape London 1935. 583 pp.
Newton, Deborah, *Virginia Woolf*. Melbourne University Press 1946. 79 pp.
Read, Herbert, *Annals on Innocence and Experience*. Faber & Faber Ltd. London 1946 (1940). 236 pp.
Richards, I. A., *Principles of Literary Criticism*. Kegan Paul, Trench, Trubner & Co. London 1925. 290 pp.
Russell, Bertrand, *What I Believe*. Kegan Paul & Co. Ltd. London 1925. 95 pp.
—»— *Autobiography: My Mental Development* vide Schilpp, P. A. (ed.), *The Philosophy of Bertrand Russell*. (The Library of Living Philosophers, vol. V.)
Sampson, George, *The Concise Cambridge History of English Literature*. Cambridge University Press 1941. XIV. 1094 pp.
Savage, D. S., *The Withered Branch*. Six Studies in the Modern Novel. Eyre & Spottiswoode London 1950. 207 pp.
Schilpp, Paul Arthur (ed.), *The Philosophy of G. E. Moore*. (The Library of Living Philosophers, vol. 4.) Northwestern University Evanston and Chicago 1942. XV. 717 pp.
—»— *The Philosophy of Bertrand Russell* (The Library of Living Philosophers, vol. 5.) Northwestern University Evanston and Chicago 1944. XV. 815 pp.
Schjelderup, Harald J., *Neuroosit ja neuroottinen luonne* (*Nevrosene og den nevrotiske karakter*, Oslo). WSOY Helsinki 1951. 174 pp.
Segura, Celia, *The Transcendental and the Transitory in Virginia Woolf's Novels*. (Argentine Association of English Culture. English Pamphlet Series No. 4.) Buenos Aires 1943. 14—17 pp.
Sitwell, Sir Osbert, *Laughter in the Next Room*. Being the fourth volume of Left Hand, Right Hand. An Autobiography. Macmillan & Co. Ltd. London 1949. 381 pp.
Spender, Stephen, *World Within World*. The Autobiography of Stephen Spender. Hamish Hamilton and the Book Society London 1951. 349 pp.
Stephen, Julia Prinsep, *Notes from Sick Rooms*. London 1883 (not available at the British Museum).
Stephen, Sir Leslie, *An Agnostic's Apology* and Other Essays. Watts & Co. London 1931 (1893) (Thinker's Library No. 19) V. 231 pp.
—»— *Essays on Freethinking and Plainspeaking*. With Introductory Essays on Leslie Stephen and His Works by James Bryce and Herbert Paul. Duckworth & Co. London 1907 (1873) LXIV. 410 pp.
—»— *Hours in a Library*. I—IV. New Edition with Additions. Smith, Elder & Co.; Duckworth & Co. 1907. X. 365 (1874. III. 381, 1876. III. 306, 1879. III. 307).

STEPHEN, SIR LESLIE, *History of English Thought in the 18th Century.* In two volumes. Smith, Elder & Co. London 1876. XVII. 466; XI. 469 pp.

—»— *Life of Henry Fawcett.* With Two Portraits. Smith, Elder & Co. London 1885 VII. 483 pp.

—»— *Sketches from Cambridge* by a Don (reprinted from the Pall Mall Gazette) London Cambridge 1865. 144 pp.

—»— *Some Early Impressions* (published in 1903 in the *National Review*) L. & V. Woolf London 1924. 192 pp.

—»— *Studies of a Biographer* in 4 vols. Duckworth & Co. London (1898. 266 pp., 1898. 284 pp., 1902. 285 pp., 1902. 279 pp).

STRACHEY, LYTTON, *Biographical Essays.* Chatto & Windus London 1948. 288 pp.

—»— *Landmarks in French Literature.* Chatto & Windus, London 1948. 156 pp.

SWINNERTON, FRANK, *The Georgian Literary Scene.* Everyman's Library No. 943. London 1946 (1938). 379 pp.

SYMONS, JULIAN, *Charles Dickens.* (The English Novelists Series.) Arthur Barker Ltd. London 1951. 94 pp.

TRILLING, LIONEL, *The Liberal Imagination.* Secker & Warburg London 1951. 303 pp.

TROY, WILLIAM, *Virginia Woolf: The Novel of Sensibility* (reprinted from The Symposium, Jan. and Apr. 1932 in Literary Opinion in America.) Essays Illustrating the Status, Methods, and Problems of Criticism in the USA since the War. Edited, with an Introduction by Morton Daumen Zabel. J. Harper & Brothers New York — London 1937. 637 pp.

VERGA, INES, *Virginia Woolf's Novels and their Analogy to Music.* English Pamphlet No. 11. Buenos Aires 1945. 6 pp.

WARD, A. C., *The Nineteen-Twenties.* Literature and Ideas in the Post-War Decade. Methuen & Co. London 1930 X. 222 pp.

WILSON, EDMUND, *Axel's Castle.* A Study in the Imaginative literature of 1870—1930. Charles Scribner's Sons. New York — London 1931. 319 pp.

WOOLF, LEONARD, *Hunting the Highbrow.* The Hogarth Press London 1927. 51 pp.

—»— *Quack, Quack!* The Hogarth Press London 1935. 201 pp.

C. *Periodicals.*

Abinger Chronicle, the, April—May 1941. Vol. 2. No. 3 pp. 23—24. *Virginia Woolf* by R. C. Trevelyan.

Cambridge Review, Oct. 17, 1942. Vol. LXIV. No. 1556 pp. 21 ff. *Virginia Woolf and the Russians* by Gilbert H. Phelps.

Criterion, Sept. 1928. Vol. VIII. No. XXX pp. 161—164. T. S. Eliot on Clive Bell's *Civilization.*

—»— Oct. 1933 Vol. XIII. No. L. pp. 78—96. *Virginia Woolf* by Robert Peel.

Dial, the, July 1921. Vol. LXXI. No. 1 pp. 101—106. *Mr. Roger Fry and the Artistic Vision* by Thomas Jewell Craven.
—»— Aug. 1921. Vol. LXXI. No. 2 p. 217. T. S. Eliot on Virginia Woolf's *Monday or Tuesday.*
—»— June 1929. Vol. LXXXVI. No. 6 pp. 518—521. *A Fanfare from Bloomsbury* by Alyse Gregory (on Clive Bell's *Civilization*).
Horizon, June 1941. Vol. III. No. 18 pp. 402—406. *Virginia Woolf* by Duncan Grant.
—»— July 1942. Vol. VI. No. 31 pp. 44—56. *Virginia Woolf* by Martin Turnell.
Listener, the, Aug. 24, 1950, pp. 279 ff. *Sense and Sensibility in Recent Writing* by Angus Wilson.
—»— March 22, 1951, pp. 465 ff. *The Legacy of the Twenties* by Noel Annan.
—»— May 10, 1951, pp. 753 ff. *The Decline of the Imagination* by Edwin Muir.
—»— Apr. 10, 1952, pp. 590 ff. *Wisdom in Madness* by John Custance.
—»— June 5, 1952, pp. 911 ff. *The Artist and Society* by Thomas Mann.
New Statesman and Nation, the, March 29, 1941. Vol. XXI. No. 527 pp. 317 ff.
Nineteenth Century and After, the, Jan. 1934. Vol. CXV. No. 683 pp. 112 ff. *Virginia Woolf* by Peter Burra.
Observer, the, Jan. 1, 1950. Harold Hobson on T. S. Eliot.
PMLA (= Publications of the Modern Language Association of America), Sept. 1946. Vol. LXI. No. 3 pp. 835 ff. *»Vision and Design» in Virginia Woolf* by John Hawley Roberts.
Saturday Review of Literature, the, Feb. 6, 1937. Vol. XV. No. 15 pp. 3—4, 14, 16. *Virginia Woolf and Feminine Fiction* by Herbert J. Muller (reprinted in *Modern Fiction*).
Scrutiny, Sept. 1938, pp. 203 ff. *»Caterpillars of the Commonwealth Unite!»* by Q. D. Leavis (on Virginia Woolf's *Three Guineas*).
—»— March 1939, pp. 404 ff. *Leslie Stephen, Cambridge Critic* by Q. D. Leavis (on Desmond MacCarthy's *Leslie Stephen*).
—»— Sept. 1949, pp. 246 ff. *Keynes, Lawrence and Cambridge* by F. R. Leavis (on Keynes' *Two Memoirs*).
Spectator, April 11, 1941. Vol. CLXVI. No. 5885 pp. 394 ff. *Virginia Woolf* by Rose Macaulay (on *The Waves*).
Times Literary Supplement, the, June 21, 1928, No. 1377 p. 465. Review on Clive Bell's *Civilization.*
—»— July 17, 1948, No. 2424 p. 401. *Bloomsbury and Beyond* (leader).
—»— July 31, 1948, No. 2426 p. 429. Correspondence by Oliver Strachey.
Valvoja, No. 6, 1951, pp. 257 ff. *E. M. Forster ja Bloomsbury* by Irma Rantavaara.

Index

The following abbreviations have been used: Virginia Woolf: VW;
Bloomsbury: Bl; footnote: fn.

Abinger Chronicle, 155 fn.
Agnostic's Apology (Stephen), 16
Aiken, Conrad, 149
Annals of Innocence and Experience (Read) 72 fn.
Annan, Noel, 11 fn., 45 fn., 51 fn., 63 fn., 65 fn., 68 fn., 73 fn., 117 fn.
Arnold, Matthew, 69
Austen, Jane, 89, 145
Beach, J. W., 84 fn., 123 fn., 135
Bell, Clive, 27, 36, 43, 44—47, 59, 64, 65 fn., 70 fn., 74 fn., 92—3, 103, 132, 143
Bell, Julian, 36
Bell, Vanessa (*née* Stephen), 20, 22, 36, 44—5, 64, 120, 123
Bennett, Arnold, 81
Bennett, Joan, 96 f., 132 fn.
Bergson, Henri, 92—3, 135, 150
Between the Acts (VW), 22, 105, 106, 150, 158—9
Birrell, Francis, 64
Blackstone, Bernard, 96 fn., 98 fn., 133
Bloomsbury, 8, 26, 44—67 *passim*, members 64, exaggeration 64 fn., views on 65 fn., attacks on 68 fn., 70 fn.; 80—83, ab. 1920 92; 95, 97 fn., and Cambridge 44, 101; and D. H. Lawrence 102—104; 126, 132, 152—53
Bowen, Elizabeth, 58, 65 fn., 98, 147, 151 fn.
Browning, Oscar, 28, 140
Burra, Peter, 152 fn.
Butler, Samuel, 17, 39, 43

Cambridge, 13—17 *passim*, 23, 26—43 *passim*, 44—5, and eccentrics 28; and friendship 41—42; and Bl. 44, 101; 47, 49, 64 fn., ideas 68 fn., 101—2; 139, 140—143, 159
Cambridge Review, Phelps on VW 93 fn., 105 fn.
Cameron, Julia (*née* Pattle) 111, 122—123
The Captain's Death-Bed and Other Essays (VW), 117 fn.
Cecil, Lord David, 97 fn.
Chambers, R. L., 96 f., 116 fn., 146 fn.
Civilization (Bell), 43, 47—59 *passim*, 132, 143
Collected Impressions (Bowen), 147 fn., 151 fn.
The Common Reader I (VW), 72, 75, 77—84 *passim*, 100, 108, 119, 123, 136, 152.
The Common Reader II (VW), 9—10, 71, 87, 113, 137
Concise Cambridge History of English Literature, 74—75 fn.
Connolly, Cyril, 51 fn.
Cornhill Magazine, 16, 18
Craven, Th. Jewell, 88 fn.
Criterion, R. Peel on VW 152 fn.
Criticism (MacCarthy), 85, 90 fn.
Cunliffe, J. W., 134
Daiches, David, 84, 95 fn., 97 fn., 116 fn., 124 fn., 135, 149
The Death of the Moth (VW), 8, 106, 121, 125, 135
Delattre, Floris, 75, 96 fn., 135 fn.
Dial, T. J. Craven on 88 fn; T. S.

Eliot on *Monday and Tuesday* 91 fn.
Dickens, Charles, 81, 151 fn.
Dickinson, G. L., 28, 29 fn., 30, 31—2; 33—43 *passim*; 101, 107
G. L. Dickinson (Forster), 34, 43
Dictionary of National Biography, 16
Drew, Elizabeth, 96 fn.
Egoist (Meredith), 11
Eliot, T. S., on élite 56 fn.; on *Civilization* 57 fn.; 58, 63, 83, 87, on *Monday and Tuesday* 91; 93, 125, 133 fn.
Enemies of Promise (Connolly), 51 fn.
English Literature between the Wars (Evans) 132 fn.
English Literature in the 20th Century (Cunliffe), 134 fn.
Essays on Free-Thinking and Plain-Speaking (Stephen), 16
Evans, B. Ifor, 132
Flush (VW), 150
The Forsyte Saga (Galsworthy), 155
Forster, E. M., 28, 34, 42—48 *passim* 51 fn., 55—6, 63, and Bl. 63 fn.; 64—5, 68 fn., 83—4, 89, 92, 96 fn., 97 fn., 101, 114, 125—6, 153
Four Quartets (Eliot), 87
Freud, Sigmund, 58, 92, 115—16, 118, 121
Fry, Roger, 28—31 *passim*, 40, 57 fn., 59, 64, 70 f., 92, 123, 150
Galsworthy, John, 81
Garnett, Constance, 92 fn.
Garnett, David, 64
The Georgian Literary Scene (Swinnerton), 44 fn., 59, 74 fn., 85 fn., 144 fn.
Good life, 29, 37, 49, 54, 75, 126—129 *passim*
Grant, Duncan, on Bl. in *Horizon* 45 fn.; 123
Gruber, Ruth, 96 fn., 133, 148
Hadfield, J. A., 118 fn.
Harrod, R. F., on Bl. 65 fn.
A Haunted House (VW), 99 fn.
Highbrow, 8, 10, 58
History of English Thought in the 18th Century (Stephen), 15
Hoare, Dorothy, 97 fn.
Hobson, Harold, on Bl. 63

The Hogarth Press, 58, 92—3, 134 fn., 139
Holtby, Winifred, 21, 96 fn.
Horizon, 74 fn.
Hours in a Library (Stephen), 17 fn., 10—12 *passim*, 23, 69, 71 fn., 72 fn., 73 fn.
Huxley, Aldous, 83—4, 93
Ibsen, Henrik, 84
Jacob's Room (VW), 43, 45 fn., 46 fn., 47 fn., 78, 82, 92, 99 fn., 100—4 *passim*, 107, 109, 125, 132
Jameson, Storm, attitude to lit. 66, 149
Johnson, Samuel, 71, 72, 77
Johnson, R. Brimley, 86 fn.
Joyce, James, 83—4, 93, 150
Keynes, John Maynard, 28, 34—36, 39, 40 fn., 43, 46—7, 64, exaggeration 64 fn.; 65, 68, 92, 103—4
Kretschmer, Ernst, 151, 153
Lawrence, D. H., 83—4, 84, 87, and Cambridge 102—104 *passim*
Lawrence, Margaret, 148
Leavis, F. R., on Keynes, Lawrence and Cambridge 64 fn.; on L. Stephen and Bl. 68 fn.; 97
Leavis, Q. D., on Bl., D. MacCarthy 68 fn.; on *Three Guineas* 68 fn., 142 fn.
Lehmann, John, 58
Lehmann, Rosamond, 58
Le roman psychologique de VW (Delattre), 75 fn., 135 fn.
Leslie Stephen Lecture (MacCarthy), 14 fn., 69 fn.
A Letter to a Young Poet (VW), 150
The Life and Letters of Leslie Stephen (Maitland), 11—16 passim, 18, 192—24
Life as we have Known It (Intr. Letter by VW), 9 f., 155
Life of Henry Fawcett (Stephen), 13, 14 fn.
Listener, Angus Wilson on VW 153 fn.; 95 fn., 108 fn.
Literary Opinion in America, Troy on VW 96 fn., 97 fn.
Lohmüller, Gertrude, 148

The Longest Journey (Forster) 43, 153
Lucas, F. L., on Bl. 66; attitude to lit. 66 fn.; 68
Macaulay, Rose, on Bl. 65 fn.; on VW 152 fn.
MacCarthy, Sir Desmond, 14 fn., 28, 43, 46, 64, attack on 68 fn.; on *The Voyage Out* and *Night and Day* 85, 90 fn.
Madame Bovary (Flaubert), 83
Maitland, F. W., 68
Mann, Thomas, 66 fn., 95 fn.
Mansfield, Katherine, 58
McTaggart, J. Mc. T. E., 28—30 *passim*, 32—35 passim, 37, 39, 41—42, 106
J. Mc. T. E. McTaggart (Dickinson) 42 fn.
Modern Fiction (VW), 81 fn., 91 fn., 99, 108
Monroe, Elizabeth, 97 fn., 113 fn., 116 fn., 149
Montaigne, M. de, 78—80 *passim*
Moore, G. E., 7, 28, 30—43 *passim*, 159
Mrs. Dalloway (VW), 82, 105—112 *passim*, 115, 116, 125, 139, 141 fn.
Muir, Edwin, 66 fn., 90 fn. on *Night and Day*
Muller, Herbert J., 97 fn., 123 fn., 131, 149
My Mental Development (B. Russell), 40 fn., 41 fn.
Meyers, F. W. H., 28, 33
Meyers, L. H., 66 fn.
The Moment and Other Essays (VW), 8 fn., 83 fn., 143 fn., 152 fn.
New Statesman and Nation, on Bl. 55, 57
Newton, Deborah, 96 fn.
Nietzsche, Friedrich, 84
Night and Day (VW), 7, 24 fn., 85, 88—91 *passim*, 105, 132, 140 fn.
Nineteenth Century and After, Burra on VW 152 fn.
The Nineteen-twenties (Ward), 135 fn., 145 fn.
Notes from Sick Rooms (Mrs. Leslie Stephen), 21

The Novel and the Modern World (Daiches), 84 fn., 95 fn., 97 fn., 116 fn.
The Novels of VW (Chambers) 146 fn.
Olivia (Dorothy Strachey Bussy), 44, 61
Orlando (VW), 25 fn., 59, 73, 106 fn., 113 fn., 118 fn., 131—138 passim, 148, 158
Peel, Robert, 152
Phelps, Gilbert H., 93
Physique and Character (Kretschmer), 151 fn.
Plato, 31, 35, 41, 43, 50, 58, 136, 143
Post-Impressionists, 58
Principia Ethica (Moore), 7, 33—39 passim, 126—7
Principles of Lit. Criticism (Richards) 39 f., 70 fn., 133 fn., 159 fn.
Proust, Marcel, 93, 144, 150
The Psychology of Men of Genius (Kretschmer), 151 fn., 153 fn.
PMLA, Robert on VW & Roger Fry 88 fn., 111
Read, Herbert, 72 fn.
Richards, I. A., 39 fn., 70 fn., 133 fn., 159
Richardson, Dorothy, 150
Roberts, J. Hawley, 88 f., 111 fn.
Roger Fry (VW), 31 fn.
A Room of One's Own (VW), 82, 84 fn., 139—149 *passim*, 155—6
Russell, Bertrand, 28, 30—37 *passim*, 40—43 *passim*, 65 fn., 92, 100, 102
Sackville-West, V., 133—135 *passim*
Sampson, Henry, 74—5
Savage, D. S. 97 fn.
Schjelderup, H. J., 118 fn.
Scrutiny, 64 fn., 68 fn., 142 fn.
Sheppard, Sir John, 28, 68 fn.
Sidgwick, Henry, 18, 28—9, 33, 41, 68 fn.
Sitwell, Sir Osbert, on Bl. 57, 59; 65
Sketches from Cambridge (Stephen), 13
Some Contemporary Novelists (Johnson), 86 fn.
Some Early Impressions (Stephen), 14 fn.
Spectator, R. Macaulay on VW 152 fn.

Spender, Stephen, 58, 63 fn., on Bl. 65 fn.
St. Ives, 22, 120—1, 132
Stephen, Adrian, 20, 45, 116 fn.
Stephen, Harriet Marian (née Thackeray), 18—19
Stephen, Julia (née Jackson), 19—22 passim, comparison to Mrs. Ramsay 112, 116, 121—125 passim, 147
Stephen, Karen, 92
Stephen, Laura, 18—19
Stephen, Sir Leslie: character 10—12, 15, 22, comparison to Mr. Ramsay 20, 23, 64 fn., 112, 117—120 passim; family 11—13; at Cambridge 13—15; attitude to religion 16, literary career 16—17; trip to America 17—18; marriage 18—19; family life 20—21; old age 23—24; 44, 64 fn., as critic 68—74, comparison with VW 76—77; 106, 114, 140, 147
Stephen, Thoby, 20, 23, 27, 45, 100
Stephen, Vanessa, see Bell, Vanessa
Stephen, Virginia, see Woolf, Virginia
Sterne, Laurence, 71, 87
Strachey, Lytton, 27, 36, 42—43, 46, 53, 63—65, 68 fn., 74 fn., 83, 92, 101, 103, 158
Strachey, Oliver, 64
Studies of a Biographer (Stephen), 69 fn.
Swinnerton, Frank, 44, 59, 74, 85, 144
Symons, J., 151 fn.
Three Guineas (VW), 68 fn., 141—149 passim, 150—156
Times, 117 fn.
Times Literary Supplement, on Bl. 56, 62—64
Tolstoy, Leo, 70, 83
To the Lighthouse (VW), 7, 19—20, 64, 82, 88, 98, 112—130
Transition (Muir), 90 fn.
Trevelyan, R. C., 155 fn.
Trilling, Lionel, 66 fn.
Troy, William, 96, 97 fn., 149, 152 fn.
The Twentieth Century Novel (Beach), 84 fn., 135 fn.

Two Memoirs (Keynes), 34, 39, 64, 68, 101, 103—4
Quack, Quack (Woolf), 21 fn., 47, 52 fn., 140 fn.
Ulysses (Joyce), 83, 93, 155
Verga, I., 155 fn.
Voltaire, 52, 83
The Voyage Out (VW), 7—10 passim, 19, 22, 26—7, 43, 60, 76, 85—7 passim, 98, 105, 114, 132, 140, 150
Ward, A. C., 135, 145
The Waves (VW), 43, 88, 106, 109, 125, 132, 150—155 passim, 159
The Way of All Flesh (Butler), 17, 39, 43
Weidner, E., 123 fn.
Wilson, Angus, 62, 153 fn., 154
Wilson, Edmund, 74 fn.
Woolf, Leonard, 27, 43, 45—47 passim, 52, 58, 64, 101, 106, 115 fn., 116 f., 139, 140
Woolf, Virginia, highbrow 8—10; personality 10, 25, 113—120, 151 fn.; appearance 19, 25, 60—1; comparison to mother 21; and religion 22, 105—7; on death 23, 61, 109—10, 121; and Cambridge 26—7, 43, 45, 100—4, 140—143; marriage 45, 39; 46, 51, 55, 58—67 passim; as critic 68—80, compared to father 76—77; on Sterne 71; on Montaigne 78; on Edwardians 81; on silence 87—8; and Russians 93—4, 120; ivory tower 95—7, 131, 149; survey on VW crit. 96—7 fn.; 98—9; nervous breakdowns 106 fn., 108—9,115 fn., 120; theory of life 88, 108—10, 125, 131—2, 157, 159; childhood, relation to parents 114—17, 123, 146—7; on human personality 119, 137; and painting 123—6; on time 135—7; and suffragettes 140—2, 157; androgynes 143—4, 148; style 145—152
The Years (VW), 27, 106, 150—58